| Semiosis Book Series 03 |

# Concession in Discourse

## Synchronic and Diachronic Analysis of English Concessives

*"Do you know that the ready concession of minor points is a part of the grace of life?"*

-Henry Harland-

**Semiosis Book Series 03**

Synchronic and Diachronic Analysis of English Concessives

# CONCESSION IN DISCOURSE

**Mikyung Ahn and Hyunsook Lee**

HU:iNE

# Concession in Discourse

– Synchronic and Diachronic Analysis of English Concessives –

by **Mikyung Ahn, Hyunsook Lee**



| | |
|---|---|
| First published | 30 May, 2016 |
| Published by | HANKUK UNIVERSITY OF FOREIGN STUDIES<br>UNIVERSITY KNOWLEDGE PRESS<br>107, Imun-ro, Dongdaemun-gu, Seoul 02450, Korea<br>Tel. 82-2-2173-2493~7, Fax. 82-2-2173-3363 |
| E-mail | press@hufs.ac.kr |
| Online | http://press.hufs.ac.kr |
| Design | EwhanD&B T. 82-2-2254-4301 |
| Print | neoprintech T. 82-2-718-3111 |
| ISBN | 979-11-5901-077-4 94740<br>978-89-7464-832-9 94080(set) |
| Price | 18,000 won |

This research was supported by Humanities Korea Project through the National Research Foundation of Korea funded by the Ministry of Education (NRF-2010-361-A00013).

# Contents

# I

# Introduction

# 1

# Introduction

Concession is considered as a conversational strategy for negotiating interlocutors' consensus as well as permitting the exchange in a conversation to be pursued (Weigand and Dascal 2001). Concession in conversation involves typically tripartite sequence of actions: First, one speaker makes a statement or a claim; second, this statement or claim is acknowledged or conceded by another speaker; third, this speaker then advances an apparently contradictory second claim or point. In collaboration these actions accomplish the more global activity of *Concession* (Couper-Kuhlen and Thompson 1999, 2000).

Concessive is a linguistic term indicating a function word that has meaning similar to anything defined as a concessive subordinator *although, while, whereas,* concessive coordinator *(al) though, but,* concessive adverbials *nevertheless, nonetheless, even so, still, yet, after all,* concessive preposition *in spite of, despite, notwithstanding,* or concessive parenthetical adverbial expressions *true enough, sure enough, admittedly.* However, concessive relationships are not necessarily marked by these markers but some sentences may also carry a concessive interpretation without overt concessive markers as in *I have to do all this work and you are watching TV* (König 1985: 2). In this study, analyzing the concessives in English, we will investigate how concession occurs in spoken discourse, in other words, how an interlocutor concedes another claim in conversation.

Concessives develop relatively late in the history of a language and are also acquired much later than other types of adverbial clauses (König 1994: 679). Nevertheless, concessives have drawn considerable attention in studies of language change and grammaticalization (König 1986; Traugott and König 1991; Chen 2000; Barth-Weingarten and Couper-Kuhlen 2002). Since these concessives are known to have developed from lexical sources across languages, looking into the process of emergence of such forms constitutes an interesting research topic for historical linguistics. Against this backdrop, the present investigation will explore the diachronic development of English concessive conjunctions.

The overall approach of the present study is qualitative and quantitative. For a qualitative approach, the current study draws on the concepts formulated in grammaticalization theory which provides a useful framework for an understanding of the historical development of English concessives. The methodology for a synchronic study is essentially quantitative. Naturally occurring data have the principal benefit of being observable and verifiable by all who care to examine it. Corpus-based observations are also intrinsically more verifiable than introspectively based judgements (McEnery and Wilson (2001[1996]: 14). To pursue the goal of corpus-based observation of English concessives, two of corpora are employed: the British National Corpus (BNC) and the Michigan Corpus of Academic Spoken English (MICASE). The BNC is a large corpus of modern English (almost 100 million words) which is designed to be a representative sampling of the language as it was used on the British Isles towards the end of the twentieth century. The MICASE consists of approximately 1.8 million words of academic speech from the university, and the speakers represented in the corpus include faculty, staff, and all levels of students, and native, near-native, and non-native speakers.

The present investigation is organized as follows: Chapter 2 discusses characteristics of concessive relations compared with the other discourse relations such as causal, contrast, corrective, and conditional, and also explores the meanings of concessives by applying Sweetser (1990)'s domain theory to them. Chapter 3 investigates how concession is realized or processed in conversation by utilizing Cardinal Concessive Schema (Couper-Kuhlen and Thomson 2000), highlighting the discourse functions of a variety of concessives. Chapter 4 provides a detailed description of present-day use of English concessives with the help of quantative data from present day English on the basis of British National Corpus

(BNC). Chapter 5 analyzes the uses of the most frequent concessive *though* as a discourse marker in spoken discourse. Chapter 6 investigates diachronic developments of English concessive conjunctions, based on the principles and mechanisms of grammaticalization theory.

# II Concessive Relations

# 2

# Concessive Relations

One who makes an utterance of the general format such as (1) is committed to the truth of both propositions (cf. König 1988: 146). Moreover, a connection is signified between the propositions of the two related clauses in question as shown in (2). In other words, the speaker utters these two propositions against the background assumption that the situations or contexts which the two propositions represent are generally incompatible. This implication involves a presupposition, not an entailment (cf. König 1986: 233). For an example such as (2), the concessive presupposition may be expressed as in (3) (Crevels 2000: 313).

(1) Although p, q

(2) Although it is raining, I am going out for a walk.

(3) If it is raining, one generally is not going out for a walk.

(Crevels 2000: 313-314)

Concessive clauses occur in all positions where adverbial clauses are allowed to occur in a language, and in many languages they may either precede or follow the main clause. However, concessive clauses have characteristics distinct from other types of adverbial clauses in many ways: "(i) in contrast to most other types of adverbial clauses, there do not seem to be many languages with a concessive interrogative pronoun analogous to English *when* (time), *why* (reason), *how* (manner) etc, (ii) concessives cannot be the focus of a focusing adjunct (focus particle) like *only, even, just, especially* (in contrast to a causal constructions as in (4a)), iii) concessives cannot occur as focus in a cleft sentence (4b); iv) concessives cannot be the focus of a negation or a polar interrogative (4c)." (König 1994: 679; Crevels 2000: 314)

(4) a .i. Only because it was raining...

ii. *Only although it was raining...

b. i. It was because it was raining that...

ii. *It was although it was raining that...

c. i. Was he harassed because he was a boxer?

ii. ?Was he harassed although he was a boxer?

(Crevels 2000: 314)

All of these divergent properties of concessive clauses seem to manifest a single syntactic/semantic constraint on their use, that is, *they cannot be focused*. This constraint generally implies that the concessive clauses are less tightly integrated into main clauses than other types of adverbial clauses (König 1994; Crevels 2000).

## 2.1 Concessive, Causal, and Conditional relations

Among adverbial relations, there is a subset whose members are associated with each other- *conditional*, *causal*, *concessive conditional* and *concessive*- and these are the label traditionally used for these relations as well as the connectives expressing these relations. Let us take a look at instances of these relation (König and Siemund 2000: 341):

(5) a. If people smoke, they will damage their health. (conditional)

b. Even if you smoke, you may become very old. (concessive conditional)

c. John's lungs are not in good shape because he smokes. (causal)

d. Even though John smokes, he still in good health. (concessive)

(König and Siemund 2000: 341)

We can arrange their four relations in a two-dimensional diagram, i.e. *hypothetical* vs. *factual* as shown in Table 1. A vertical division distinguishes relations in accordance with whether those are factual or hypothetical. The horizontal division distinguishes relations whose arguments are in harmony with general tendencies. In other words, the relations in the horizontal division describe typical sequences of situations or a typical concomitance of situations in the world, or express a dissonance with general regularities of co-occurrence (König and Siemund 2000: 341-342).

Table 1. Sense relations

| | Hypothetical | Factual |
|---|---|---|
| Harmony | conditional | causal |
| Dissonance | concessive conditional | concessive |

(König and Siemund 2000: 342)

As shown in Table 1, there are similarities in the formal expression between conditionals and causals, on the one hand, and between concessive conditionals and concessives on the other hand. Languages may express the vertical aspects of relatedness and code causals and concessives in similar fashion. They also employ similar formal device for conditionals and concessive conditionals. Given sense relations in Table 1, there seems no similarity in the expression of causal constructions and concessive conditionals. In this regard, typological studies on adverbial relations can be based on the criterion of whether languages give priority to the horizontal or vertical relations (König and Siemund 2000: 342).

Concessive conditionals can develop into concessives or can be employed as concessives whenever the truth of the antecedent is contextually given (cf. (6a)). English *though* still had a concessive conditional meaning ('even if') in Early Modern English as shown in (6b) (König and Siemund 2000: 343).

(6) a. Even if you dislike museums-which I know you do-the Museum of Modern Art is worth a visit.

b. I'll speak to it though hell itself should gape and bid me hold my peace. (sh. Hamlet I.ii 244)

(König and Siemund 2000: 343)

These specific types of relatedness can be summarized as follows (cf. Kortmann, 1997: 197ff):

(7) a. causal constructions presuppose conditionals

b. conditionals can be elaborated, enriched to concessive conditionals

c. concessive conditionals may change into concessives

(König and Siemund 2000: 343)

According to König, concessive clauses and complex concessive sentences are infrequently used for the speech act or speech activity of conceding. Moreover, they suggest that labels like the following would be much more appropriate than concessives: "incausal", "inoperant cause", "anticause", "cause contraire", "condition contrecarre", etc. (König and Siemund 2000: 343). However, there is the assumption that some relation of opposition between causal and concessive constructions can be posed and supported solely based on clear intuitions. The intuition that concessive relations are semantically the opposite of causal relations is simply mentioned rather than fully explained (cf. Hermodsson 1973, 1994; Azar 1997; König and Siemund 2000: 347).

According to Di Meola (1998), concessive relations do not involve only one underlying causal relation but there are two such relations operating in the background. The following example can be used to illustrate this idea (König and Siemund 2000: 347-348).

(8) Although Carol is ill, she goes to work today.

(9) A: Since Carol is ill, she cannot go to work.

B: Since there is an important business meeting today, Carol goes to work.

(König and Siemund 2000: 348)

Di Meola (1998) suggests that this concessive construction in (8) is based on the hypothetical causal relation given in (9A) as well as on the relation in (9B). The relations expressed in (9) amount to the schema given below (cf. Di Meola 1998: 338; König and Siemund 2000: 348).

(10) A1: being ill → A2: not go to work

B1: important business meeting → B2: go to work

(König and Siemund 2000: 348)

While the antecedents are ordered hierarchically, the consequents of these two causal relations are mutually exclusive. The interesting point about these concessive relations is that two causes compete with each other and that the stronger or more significant one wins out (B1 in (10)). According to Di Meola (1998), concessive constructions code antecedent and consequent of two different causal relations, and the 'successful' cause (B1 in (10)) is almost never linguistically coded, where concessivity is defined as "hidden causality" (König and Siemund 2000: 348).

There appear to be concessive relations without "hidden causes". König and Siemund (2000) claim that it is not possible to assume double causality (in (11a)). In other words, they claim that it is impossible to reconstruct a conceivable cause why the flat is located in a nice area, saying that various stipulations are needed to explain them within this framework (König and Siemund 2000: 348).

(11) a. Although the flat is too small, it is located in a nice area

b. He was laughing, although he was desperate.

c. The ostrich is a bird, although it cannot fly.

(König and Siemund 2000: 348)

The following examples (12a-d) also reveal the problems of Di Meola's theory. General assumptions of plausibility about the interrelation of events in (12) are violated: for instance, expensive flats are normally well-equipped (12a) and they are easily explained within more traditional framework of concessive relations. It seems quite difficult to reconstruct a hidden cause. In (12b) also, it is not easy to recover a cause for the bad taste for the pizza. Thus, the symmetrical nature of Di Meola's analysis looks very appealing but examples like (12) make one wonder whether it is plausible that concessive constructions encode a "hidden cause" (König and Siemund 2000: 349).

(12) a. Although the flat is expensive, it is not well-equipped.

b. Although the pizza is expensive, it does not taste good.

c. Although the programme is bad, many people watch television.

d. Although he has a lot of money, he does not feel happy.

(König and Siemund 2000: 349)

To avoid all these problems, Di Meola's analysis need to be restricted to what Sweetser calls linking at the content level (Azar's 1997 "indirect-rejection concessivity"). Then the example (11) might be excluded as potential counterexamples. Nevertheless, as for this subset of concessive constructions, there is a fundamental problem: "a sentence like (12b) can never give rise to a conversational inference for which propositions like 'the pizza is cheap/old...' are used as a premise" (König and Siemund 2000: 349). Di meola (1998) also does not provide basic semantic outlines contextually. Moreover, there is another problematic view that concessive constructions are somehow noncooperative, as revealed by "hidden causality." (König and Siemund 2000: 349)

## 2.2 Contrast, Concessive, and Corrective

Previous studies on discourse connectives or discourse markers have contributed much to our understanding of the uses and meanings of connectives of opposition. As mentioned in the previous section, however, there still has been a lack of consensus on the classification of opposition relations. The opposition relations have been classified in different ways and have been variously termed in the previous literature: “contrast”, “contrastive”, “concessive”, “concession”, “adversative” “corrective”, “substitutive” (Jespersen 1940; Halliday and Hasan 1976; Quirk et al. 1985; Leech 1989 and others; Izutsu 2008: 647).

Most of studies on opposition relations can be largely classified into two groups, i.e. ‘the contrast and concessive dichotomy’ (Lakoff 1971; Blackmore 1987, 1989; Spooren 1989; Kehler 2002) and ‘the corrective and non corrective dichotomy’ (Anscombre and Ducrot 1977; Dascal and Katriel 1977; Abraham 1979; Lang 1984; Foolen 1991; von Klopp 1994; Winter and Rimon 1994). The first group highlights clarifying the semantic distinction between a simple contrast and the concessive meaning. The second group focuses on the classification of coordinate conjunctions into SN-type (adopted from Spanish *sino* and German *sondern*) and PA-type (from Spanish *pero* and German *aber*). The SN-type conjunctions express some kind of correction with the meaning of “not...but...” and the PA-type conjunctions cover the semantic areas of both simple contrast and concessive without a clear distinction between them (Izutsu 2008: 648).

Izutsu (2008) classifies opposition relations into three semantic categories: contrast, concessive, and corrective, as shown in (13)-(15) respectively:

(13) Contrast

a. John is rich, but Tom is poor

b. I’ve read sixty pages, whereas she’s read only twenty.

c. John likes math, Bill likes music, while Tom likes chemistry.

(Izutsu 2008: 648)

(14) Concessive

a. Although John is poor, he is happy

b. Bill studies hard, but he failed the exam

c. We thought it would rain; nevertheless, we went for a walk.

(Izutsu 2008: 649)

(15) Corrective

a. John is not American but British.

b. Ann doesn't like coffee-she likes tea

c. My grandmother died in 1978, (and) not 1977.

(Izutsu 2008: 649)

Foolen (1991) has already discussed this triadic classification by analyzing multiple uses of conjunctions in some languages (English *but*, Russian *a*, Hebrew *ala*). He classifies the opposition relations into three types, i.e. semantic opposition, denial of expectation, and correction, which correspond contrast, concessive and corrective respectively. His first two types have been adopted from Lakoff's distinction between semantic opposition and denial of expectation and the third type have been taken from the lexical distinction between *aber* and *sondern* in German, of which *sondern* is solely employed for corrective (Izutsu 2008: 649).

The contrast meaning in English is signified by adverbial connectives such as *in/by contrast, conversely,* and *by comparison,* as in (16).

The English concessive meaning is implied by subordinate conjunctions such as *although* and *even if* or by adverbial connectives such as *nevertheless* and *nonetheless* as in (17) (Izutsu 2008: 652).

(16) a. Light industries, like textiles, are expanding rapidly. *In contrast*, heavy industries, like mining, are in decline.

b. Between 1990 and 2000, Seattle Power's residential customers saw rates increase by 26 percent. *By comparison*, the rates of Portland Gas & Electric rose 38 percent.

c. Male lions may sometimes attack young lion cubs. *Conversely*, female lions will attack male lions to protect their young.

(Izutsu 2008: 652).

(17) a. *Although* John is poor, he is happy.

b. *Though* Mary is very ill, she is quite conscious.

c. I'll go out *even if* it rains.

d. *Notwithstanding* that there is very little reason of being optimistic at this moment, you can see some hope.

e. We thought it would rain; *nevertheless/nonetheless*, we went for a walk.

f. Bill worked hard, *and yet* he failed.

(Izutsu 2008: 652).

The corrective meaning is signalled by the insertion of *instead* or *rather* as shown in (18). The sentence *Mary is not stupid but ugly* is ambiguous between the concessive and corrective interpretations. The former interpretation can be analyzed as Mary is [not stupid] but [ugly], while the latter is taken as Mary is not [stupid] but [lazy] (Izutsu 2008: 652).

(18) Mary is not stupid, but instead (or rather) ugly.

(cf. Pusch 1975: 58; Izutsu 2008: 652)

Lakoff (1971) has pointed out that three categories also exhibit distinct syntactic behaviors. The contrast sentence such as *John is rich, but Tom is poor* in (19) does not represent a significant change in meaning after reversing the order of clauses in (19a), paraphrasing with *and* in (19b), and omitting the connective as in (19c), in concessive and corrective. However, these syntactic operations cause semantic or syntactic changes in concessive constructions (Izutsu 2008: 653).

(19) a. Tom is poor, but John is rich.

b. John is rich, and Tom is poor.

c. John is poor; Tom is poor.

(Izutsu 2008: 653)

The meaning of the sentence *Although John is poor, he is happy* in (14a) changes if the order of two clauses is reversed as in (20a). In (14a), what the speaker asserts is *John is happy* whereas in (20a) the speaker asserts that *John is poor.* In (20b) where the sentence is paraphrased with *and,* the sentence does not express the concessive interpretation. In (20c), where the connective is omitted, the sentence is no longer represents concessive meaning. The two sentences simply state the occurrence of two situations but are not associated with the concessive meaning (Izutsu 2008: 653).

(20) a. Although John is happy, he is poor.

b. John is poor, and he is happy.

c. John is poor; he is happy.

(Izutsu 2008: 653)

For corrective, as the order of the two conjuncts is reversed, the meaning of corrective sentence *John is not American but British* in (15a) also dramatically changes as in (21a). If the sentence is paraphrased with *and,* as in (21b), it becomes less felicitous. In (21c) where the connective is left out, the sentence is less felicitous as well (Izutsu 2008).

(21) a. John is not British but American

b. ? John is not American and British.

c. ? John is not American, British.

(Izutsu 2008: 653)

Contrast and concessive are also different in terms of gapping and pronoun interpretation (Kehler 2002). Gapping is felicitious in the contrast relation as in (22a), but it is infelicitious with the concessive interpretation as in (22b):

(22) a. The boys voted today. John voted for Gore, but (in contrast) Tom for Bush.

b. Tom usually does everything that John does, but not today. #John voted for Gore, but (surprisingly) Tom for Bush.

(Kehler 2002: 84; Izutsu 2008: 653)

Pronoun interpretation also shows a similar difference: whereas contrast guarantees the interpretation, concession does not preserve it. Contrast follows 'parallel function strategy' (e.g. Sheldon 1974; Grober et al. 1978). In (23), contrast preserves the interpretation that a pronoun *him* in the second conjunct is co-referential with the NP (=Dave) that has the same grammatical role in the first conjunct(Izutsu 2008: 654).

(23) a. Simon bullied Dave, but (in contrast) Ken sympathized with him(him=Dave)

b. Simon bullied Dave, but (nevertheless) Ken sympathized with him. (him=Simon or Dave)

(Izutsu 2008: 654)

However, concessive sentences do not conform to the parallel function strategy. In (23) the pronoun *him* can refer to Simon or Dave, depending on the interpretation of the sentence: if the speaker thinks Simon to be a school bully who has difficulty in getting along with classmates, the pronoun will refer to Simon. On the other hand, suppose that the speaker knows Simon and Ken to be friends who get along with each other well, the pronoun can refer to Dave (Izutsu 2008: 654).

## 2.3 Concessives on Different Semantic Levels

Sweetser (1990) analyzes and classifies multiple uses of modal verbs and conjunctions into three different types of entities, i.e. (i) real or hypothetical situations, (ii) aspects of knowledge or (iii) speech acts. The different entities above occur at the content, the epistemic or the illocutionary level respectively. These distinctions may also be applied to concessive constructions and Sweetser's semantic domains correspond, respectively, to the predicational, the propositional and the illocutionary layers within the layered structure of the clause in Functional Grammar (cf. Dik et al. 1990; Crevels 1994, 1998, 2000). In Functional Grammar, it is conceived that layers of higher complexity fully contain those of higher complexity, and in other words, every speech act contains a proposition and every proposition contains a predication. In addition to three layers proposed by Sweetser (1990), a fourth layer, the so-called text layer (Crevels 1994, 1998, 2000; Hengeveld 1997) is needed. Concessive clauses pertaining to this text layer are associated with the organization of the discourse, and apply to text units which may contain more than one sentence (Crevels 2000: 315).

In Functional Grammar, it is claimed that six layers are relevant for the analysis of clause structure (Hengeveld 1989, 1992, 1997; Crevels 1994, 1998, 2000). According to Hengeveld (1996: 119), it may be problematic to provide evidence for the validity of these layers in main clauses. A better solution to this problem is to study the properties of subordinate constructions rather than main clauses. Since each of the layers present in the hierarchical clause model may be applied to a subordinate construction, the study of diverse layers of subordinate clauses will help understand the differences between the layers (Crevels 2000: 315).

A strong evidence supporting the existence of the different semantic levels is that languages may use different conjunctions to express the same kind of adverbial relation. For causal relations, French *parce que* 'because' is employed specifically for content domain, while *puisque* is used at the epistemic or illocutionary level (cf. Sweetser 1990: 82, 156). Latin *quoniam*, English *since*, and Spanish *ya que* are also employed for an epistemic or speech-act domain rather than content one (Quirk et al. 1985; Bolkestein 1991; Crevels 1994, 1998, 2000: 315-316).

A concessive relation in the content domain implies that although the event or the state of affairs described in the concessive clause poses an obstacle for the event or the state of affairs in the main clause, it does not impede its realization as shown in (24) (Crevels 2000: 318).

(24) She's just given birth to a beautiful baby girl although she's fifty two.

(Crevels 2000: 318)

A concessive relation in the epistemic domain implies that the speaker, despite being convinced of the content of the concessive clause, still reaches the opposite conclusion contained in the main clause. As shown in (25), a concessive conjunction in the epistemic domain will mark the impediment of a belief or a conclusion. In other words, a concessive relation in the epistemic domain does not represent any factual conflict but a conflict between the conclusion and the potential counterargument contained in the concessive clause (Crevels 2000: 318).

(25) He left his wife and children although he loved them very much.

(26) Although it's none of my business, your behavior is a disgrace

(Crevels 2000: 318)

On the other hand, a concessive relation in the speech-act domain does not impede the realization of the event or the state of affairs contained in the main clause, but forms obstacles for the realization of the speech act expressed by the speaker in the main clause as shown in (26). An intended meaning of (26) could be understood such as 'I know that I have no business commenting on your behaviour, so I normally wouldn't do so' or 'I know that I have no business commenting on your behaviour, so normally wouldn't perform the speech act of commenting on it.' (Crevels 2000: 318)

Lastly, in contrast to a concessive in the speech act domain, a concessive in the textual domain does not modify the main clause of a concessive construction, but generally influences a whole preceding text unit. While a concessive in speech act domain is always part of a single construction, and therefore, specifies or modifies a single preceding or following speech act, a concessive in the text domain usually modifies a whole series of preceding propositions, and often plays a role as an afterthought as shown in (27) (Crevels 2000: 319).

> (27) My favourite poster is, a French one for Nesquik, which shows a sophisticated-looking small boy leaning nonchalantly against something and saying that thanks to Nesquik he went back on to milk. He really looks a nice child. Though, there are some children that one would feel quite a shamed to have around the house...
>
> (Greenbaum 1969: 68; Crevels 2000: 319)

Worth noting that in written language one may be confronted with the bias of punctuation conventions, but textual concessive clauses do not always occur in the form of a simple sentence. In addition, textual concessive clauses typically exhibit main clause word order in those languages like Dutch and German (König and van der Auwera 1988, Gunthner 1993; Crevels 2000: 319).

Thus, different subtypes of concessive clauses show different degrees of integration into a main clause. Concessive clauses cannot be focused and generally take wide scope over any operator in the main clause. In that regard, it can be concluded that a concessive clause is less tightly connected to a main clause than a conditional, temporal or causal clause. The higher the semantic level of a concessive clause is the looser it is be integrated into a main clause and the more paratactic-like it is (Crevels 2000: 320).

The application of Sweetser's approach to the concessives, however, may pose a conceptual dilemma. The examples like (30) and (31) seem to be clear negative parallels to (28) and (29) (Verhagen 2000: 362-363).

(28) John passed his exams because he worked hard.

(29) John worked hard, because he passed his exams.

(30) John did not pass his exams although he worked hard.

(31) John did not work hard, although he passed his exams.

(Verhagen 2000: 363)

In example (30), the real-world causal connection between *passing exams* and *working hard* is negated, leading to a case of concession in the content domain. Similarily, in (31) the validity of the inference from the knowledge of *John's passing his exams* is negated, and therefore, this could be a case of concession in the epistemic domain (cf. the examples and paraphrases of 'adversative' conjunctions in Sweetser 1990: 79). Interesting noting if the concessive is the negative counterpart of the causal, we could expect the domain theory to be applicable in a parallel fashion in the distinct domains (Verhagen 2000: 364).

However, Sweetser (1990) points out that for the adversative conjunction *but,* which is even more general and semantically simpler than concessive *although*, it is hard to find clear examples of content usages. A contrastive relation always goes through a construal as a relation of reasoning, involving relations between arguments and conclusions, and therefore, it is not restricted to real-world relations (Verhagen 2000: 364).

(32) John worked hard, *but* he did not pass his exams.

(Verhagen 2000: 364)

The contrast implied by *but* in (32) cannot be sufficiently explained in terms of the real world facts of *working hard* and *not passing,* because these situations can be compatible in the real world, that is, they co-occur quite often. In order to explain the contrast, it is needed to "invoke some reasoning process on the basis of general and specific knowledge licensing the expectation that John could pass his exams, so that the contrast can be construed as holding between this expectation and the actual fact of John's failing" (Verhagen 2000: 364).

In other words, it is not quite clear what the content of the concept 'contrast' should be in the real world without referring to some person perceiving or conceptualizing a contrast (Sweetser 1990: 103-104). If we regard the use of *but* as inherently epistemic because the concept 'contrast' requires reference to reasoning, we could also consider *although* inherently epistemic as well, for it is also related to contrast. The example (30) signified by *although* is as contrastive as (32) implied by *but,* and therefore, it requires reference to the same kind of unfulfilled expectations or reasoning (Verhagen 2000: 364).

## 2.4 Contrast and Concessive as a Rhetorical Relation

Contrast is a central rhetorical relation, which is one of the most frequent relations. It has been claimed to have a clear, intuitive semantic meaning and to interact with other linguistic structures (see e.g. Kehler 2000). Contrast is also related to discourse markers such as *however, although* and *but*. However, there has not been general consensus about whether there are qualitatively different contrast relations or not. Rhetorical Structure Theory recognizes three different types: *contrast, antithesis* and *concession*. Wolf and Gibson (2005) recognize two relations, i.e. *denial of expectation* and *contrast*, whereas Segmented Discourse Representation Theory (SDRT, Asher and Lascarides 2003) recognizes solely one relation, i.e. *contrast* (Spenader and Labanova 2009: 211).

Theoretically, Rhetorical Structure Theory(RST) is associated with 78 relations in the manually annotated RST corpus (Carlson et al. 2003) including three contrast relations: *contrast, antithesis*, and *concession*. Wolf and Gibson (2005) identify two contrast relations among the 11 relations, i.e. 'violated expectation' and 'contrast', which seems to have been taken from Hobbs (1985) and Lakoff (1971). Reese et al. (2007) recognize only one *contrast* relation among the 14 relations, following the annotation of texts according to SDRT. Thus, RST recognizes a number of contrast types. The distinctions between these contrast types in current discourse annotation schemes seem to have been adapted from theoretical linguistic work on contrast. For instance, in the uses of *but*, Lakoff

(1971) made a distinction between what she called *denial of expectation* and *semantic opposition* (Spenader and Labanova 2009: 211).

(33) It's raining but I'm taking an umbrella

(34) John is tall but Bill is short

(Lakoff 1971: 133; Spenader and Labanova 2009: 211)

Denial of expectation can be understood as "a case where the first conjunct implicates a proposition that the second conjunct denies." For instance, as shown in (33), "It's raining" implicates the speaker will get wet, whereas having an umbrella denies this implication. On the other hand, semantic opposition implies that the conjuncts allow parallel elements to contrast along one dimension: For example, as in (34), *John and Bill* are contrasted in terms of their height (Spenader and Labanova 2009: 211).

The three RST relations have the similar distinction. Antithesis and contrast seem to have contrast in only one or few respects (Carlson and Marcu 2001), and clearly reflect the definition of semantic opposition: antithesis and contrast only have contrast in terms of symmetry, which is realized in terms of nucleus in RST. Whereas in multinuclear contrast, the nucleuses of conjuncts should not be more prominent, nor more associated with the rest of the discourse, in a mononuclear antithesis relation, the nucleus can be more prominent as shown in the examples below (Spenader and Labanova 2009: 212).

(35) Antithesis

Although Exxon spent heavily during the latest quarter to clean up the Alaskan shoreline blackened by its huge oil spill, those expenses as well as the cost of a continuing spill-related program are covered by $880 million in charges taken during the first half

(wsj 1311; extracted from Spenader and Labanova 2009: 212)

(36) Antithesis

A hearing is set for Nov. 15, but participants don't expect a resolution until July 1990.

(wsj 1145; extracted from Spenader and Labanova 2009: 212)

(37) Contrast

Import values are calculated on a cost, insurance and freight basis, while exports are accounted for on a free-on-board basis

(wsj 0615; extracted from Spenader and Labanova 2009: 212)

(38) Contrast

The clash of ideologies survives this treatment, but the nuance and richness of Gorky's individual characters have vanished in the scuffle.

(wsj0615; extracted from Spenader and Labanova 2009: 212)

On the other hand, in a concession relation, there is no kind of parallel elements typical of contrast and antithesis, and the contrast seems to be the result of an unexpected situation and is related to a denial of expectation as follows (Spenader and Labanova 2009: 212):

"The situation indicated in the nucleus is contrary to expectation in the light of the information presented in the satellite. In other words, a CONCESSION relation is always characterized by a violated expectation. (Compare to ANTITHESIS). In some cases, which text span is the satellite and which is the nucleus do not depend on the semantics of the spans, but rather on the intention of the writer." (Annotation manual, Carlson and Marcu, 2001; Spenader and Labanova, 2009: 212)

Contrast constructions such as example (37) and (38) show parallel elements but in many ways, antithesis in (36) seems to have common with concession in (40). For concession in (39), the brokerage operation and Kidder are parallel elements without comparison of profits or losses.

(39) Concession

Its 1400-member brokerage operation reported an estimated $5 million loss last year, although Kidder expects it to turn a profit this year

(ws0604; extracted from Spenader and Labanova 2009: 213)

(40) Concession

While there have been no reports of similar sudden unexplained deaths among diabetics in the U.S., Dr. Sobel said the FDA plans to examine Dr. Toseland's evidence and is considering its own study here.

(ws0690; extracted from Spenader and Labanova 2009: 213)

For analysis of the three-way distinction of contrast relations, i.e.

contrast, antithesis and concession, Spenader and Labanova (2009) used the annotated RST corpus as data, and this corpus has approximately 176,000 words comprising 385 articles from the Wall Street Journal portion of the Penn Tree bank. They extracted all contrast, antithesis, concession, evidence, cause and result relations from the RST corpus (Spenader and Labanova 2009: 216).

Table 2. Set of three Contrast relations compared with three Cause-Effect relations. (Spenader and Labanova 2009: 216)

| | | Contrast set (%) | Cause-Effect set (%) |
|---|---|---|---|
| p | though | 0.11 | 0.05 |
| | even | 0.18 | 0.11 |
| | despite | 0.06 | 0.02 |
| p | although | 0.10 | 0.02 |
| p | but | 0.85 | 0.44 |
| | however | 0.09 | 0.06 |
| p | still | 0.14 | 0.05 |
| p | while | 0.15 | 0.09 |
| | only | 0.15 | 0.17 |
| | too | 0.08 | 0.04 |

As seen in Table 2, many typical markers of contrast actually distinguish contrast relations from cause-effect relations. A typical marker of contrast is not significantly more frequent in contrast than in cause-effect relations. Worth noticing that many lexical items, not generally considered as discourse markers, i.e. *even*, *still* are in fact frequently used (Spenader and Labanova 2009: 215).

Table 3. Nuclearity compared: Mononu-clear Antithesis and Concession com-pared with multinuclear Contrast.(Spenader and Labanova 2009: 217)

| | | Antithesis+Concesssion (%) | Contrast (%) |
|---|---|---|---|
| p | though | **0.16** | 0.05 |
| p | even | **0.22** | 0.13 |
| p | despite | **0.08** | 0.03 |
| p | although | **0.15** | 0.04 |
| | but | 0.85 | 0.44 |
| | however | 0.09 | 0.06 |
| | still | **0.17** | 0.11 |
| | while | **0.18** | 0.12 |
| | only | 0.17 | 0.13 |
| | too | 0.09 | 0.04 |

The three contrast relations may be grouped along two features, that is to say, their nuclearity and the way in which they construe the contrast, antithesis, and concession are both mononuclear relations whereas contrast is multinuclear. As shown in Table 3, *but* and *too* mark antithesis and concession equally to contrast. A number of markers such as *though, although, despite, even, still,* and *while,* which are used for distinguishing contrast from cause-effect relations, are also useful for distinguishing antithesis and concession from contrast (Spenader and Labanova 2009: 217).

Table 4 shows that the typical markers such as *though, although, even, despite*, and *only* distinguish concession from antithesis and contrast. These results from Table 3, Table 4, and Table 5 suggest that concession is quite different from antithesis and contrast. The markers such as *though, even*, and *despite* distinguish concession

Table 4. Contrast types compared: An-tithesis and Contrast versus Concession. (Spenader and Labanova 2009: 217)

| | | Antithesis+Concesssion (%) | Contrast (%) |
|---|---|---|---|
| p | though | 0.07 | **0.27** |
| p | even | 0.14 | **0.33** |
| p | despite | 0.04 | **0.13** |
| p | although | 0.08 | **0.17** |
| | **but** | **0.89** | 0.44 |
| | however | 0.09 | 0.08 |
| | still | 0.13 | 0.18 |
| | while | 0.16 | 0.14 |
| | **only** | 0.14 | **0.22** |
| | too | 0.08 | 0.06 |

Table 5. Antithesis compared with Con-cession(Spenader and Labanova 2009: 218)

| | | Antithesis (%) | Concession (%) |
|---|---|---|---|
| p | though | 0.10 | **0.27** |
| p | even | 0.15 | **0.33** |
| p | despite | 0.05 | **0.13** |
| | although | 0.14 | 0.17 |
| | **but** | **0.93** | 0.72 |
| | however | 0.12 | 0.08 |
| | still | 0.16 | 0.18 |
| | while | 0.20 | 0.15 |
| | only | 0.14 | 0.22 |
| | too | 0.10 | 0.06 |

from antithesis and concession from contrast, and therefore, they are actually just markers of concession. Table 6 displays that since *although* distinguishes concession from contrast but it does not distinguish antithesis from concession, it represents antithesis as well as concession (Spenader and Labanova 2009: 217-218).

Table 6. Contrast compared with Concession(Spenader and Labanova 2009: 218)

| | | Contrast (%) | Concession (%) |
|---|---|---|---|
| p | though | 0.05 | **0.27** |
| p | even | 0.13 | **0.33** |
| p | despite | 0.03 | **0.13** |
| p | although | 0.04 | **0.17** |
| | but | 0.86 | 0.72 |
| | however | 0.08 | 0.08 |
| | still | 0.11 | **0.18** |
| | while | 0.12 | 0.15 |
| | only | 0.13 | **0.22** |
| | too | 0.07 | 0.06 |

In terms of the discourse markers, concession differs from antithesis and contrast, which implies that the way in which the contrast relation is construed is more related to lexical marking choices than nuclearity or symmetry. Worth noting that the reliable discourse markers are distinguished from those in the annotation manual: *although* and *despite* mostly characterizes concession, not antithesis and *however* is not a reliable marker of contrast relations when compared with cause-effect relations. Nevertheless, *however* is a reliable indicator of contrast when it distinguishes contrast from narration (Spenader and Labanova 2009: 218-219).

# III

# The Cardinal Concessive

# 3

# The Cardinal Concessive

## 3.1 The Cardinal Concessive

Elizabeth Couper-Kuhlen and Sandra A. Thomson (2000) propose that a Cardinal Concessive can be defined in abstract terms and used as a reference schema for actual instantiation in conversation. The schema consists of three parts which we represent with X, X′ and Y. The schema is realized verbally, and are maximally distinctive with respect to other possible hypotactic clause combinations. The pattern shown in example (41) below is an example of a Cardinal Concessive and could be represented provisionally as shown in (41′) (Couper-Kuhlen and Thomson 2000: 385).

(41) Joanne and Leonore are discussing a mutual friend who has engaged in a substance abuse.

Joanne: but he's healthy as on OX,
that guy.
(---) (h) that guy is HEAL [ THY as an o:x.
a Leonore: [his liver,
a → except for his liver.
Joanne: (-) yeah,
but I'm saying,
is like
you know,
b → as much as he's ABU:SED his liver
and all other (-) other things in his life,
he's still HEALTHY as an OX.

(Couper-Kuhlen and Thomson 2000: 381)

(41′) Schematic representation of Cardinal Concessive in (1) (provisional)

A: X That guy's liver is not healthy
B: X′ As much as he's abused his liver (He's abused his liver a lot)
Y He's still healthy as an ox

(Couper-Kuhlen and Thomson 2000: 385)

(41″) Schematic representation of Cardinal Concessive

A: X
B: X′
Y

(where X and Y are understood by participants as potentially contrasting)

(Couper-Kuhlen and Thomson 2000: 385)

Example (42) shows another important dimension of conversational conceding. Again, we have labeled the moves we understand the speakers to be making with X, X′ and Y (Couper-Kuhlen and Thomson 2000: 385).

(42) Charles and Steve, currently in NYC, are lamenting the advent of Starbuck's coffeehouses, which Steve says will 'blow out' the small privately owned places in cities like Minneapolis.

| | | |
|---|---|---|
| X | Charles: | but even the privately owned places here- HERE, |
| X | | are so CHARACTERLESS, |
| | | (-) I mean by and large. |
| X′ | Steve: | (--) OUTSIDE [ of the Village they are |
| | Charlers: | [you know. |
| Y | Steve: | (--) ther's [some in the Village that are nice. |
| | Charles: | [outside of the Village, yeah. |
| | | yeah, |
| | | that you certainly wouldn't wanna lose. |
| | | but everywhere ELSE, |
| | | you know they're all like, |
| | | CHRO:ME and BLACK [(  ) CHAIRS, |
| | Steve: | [oh up here it's horrible. |
| | Charles: | and (    ) pictures and so forth. |

15 Steve: yeah, they OBVIOUS-
they're not places where they want you to
LINGER.
(Couper-Kuhlen and Thomson 2000: 385-386)

In lines 1-2, Charles argues that even the privately owned coffeehouses here are so characterless. When Steve does not immediately support this judgement, Charles downgrades it somewhat by adding *by and large* (line 3). In the next turn, Steve acknowledges that Charles' judgement is partially true, saying that privately owned places outside Greenwich Village are indeed characterless (line 4). However, he continues arguing that there are privately owned and nice places in the Village (line 6), which implies that Charles' claim is wrong (Couper-Kuhlen and Thomson 2000: 386).

A significant feature of this example is the nature of the conceding move, labeled X′ at line 4. In other words, in his conceding move, Steve makes a contrast between two aspects of a single proposition, called 'partitioning'. Steve acknowledges that privately owned coffeehouses outside of the Village are characterless, but there's some in the Village that are nice. Worth noticing that speakers often do conceding by acknowledging only part of what the other speakers have said. A speaker concedes another's point by acknowledging part of it (Couper-Kuhlen and Thomson 2000: 386).

This interaction can be represented in terms of the Cardinal Concessive schema as shown in (42′).

(42′) Schematic representation of Cardinal Concessive in (2) (provisional)

A: X The privately owned places here are so characterless

B: X′ Outside the Village they are

Y There's some in the Village that are nice.

(where X and Y are understood by participants as potentially contrasting)

(Couper-Kuhlen and Thomson 2000: 387)

Let us take a look at another excerpt. In (43), Bee creates the first part of a Concessive schema, i.e. the X of the Cardinal Concessive schema in line 2. Ava jokingly concedes that she is home, which means Bee is partially right (X′). She does this conceding by partitioning Bee's X just as Steve does in example (42). By acknowledging Bee's remark partially (X′), Ava can set up a contrast between 'physically' and 'not physically', and Bee can collaboratively provide the Y of the Cardinal Concessive Schema, that is, 'she is not home mentally'(Couper-Kuhlen and Thomson 2000: 387).

(43) Bee and Ava (on the phone) have been joking about each other's knowledge of where the other is.

Bee: I FINALLY said something right.

X (0.2) YOU ARE HOME. (hhhh)

X′ Ava: yeah- I BELIEVE so.

X′ PHYSICALLY anyway.

Bee: yea:h.

not MENTALLY (h) though. (hh)

(Couper-Kuhlen and Thomson 2000: 387)

Thus, it is the shared knowledge of and familarity with the Cardinal Concessive schema that enables interlocutors to collaborate in the joint production of this pattern (Couper-Kuhlen and Thomson 2000: 388).

In addition to its interactional reality, the Cardinal Concessive schema has two advantages as an analytic tool. First, the Cardinal Concessive schema provides for maximal flexibility in the lexico-syntactic forms of its constituent parts. Second, it underspecifies the linkage between X′ and Y. The Cardinal Concessive schema allows for its constituent parts X, X′ and Y to be realized by a variety of linguistic units such as words, phrases, clauses or whole chunks of discourse. The examples (41)-(43) show all three parts of the Cardinal Concessive schema were phrases or clauses whereas in example (44), it is realized by a single word, *yeah* (Couper-Kuhlen and Thomson 2000: 388)

(44) Marie has called in to this Berkeley radio phone-in program during the 1991 Gulf War to talk about an anti-war demonstration which took place the day before and in which she took part. The demonstration erupted into violence.

1 Marie: I DO -I DO wanna say
that I really think a lot of people were
SINCERELY there,
just to make the opinion KNOWN that,
(0.7) it was STILL time to negotiate,

| | | |
|---|---|---|
| | | and we didn't need to start the BOMBING. |
| X | | and (0.6) I hate to SEE: uhm, |
| X | | (0.3) EVERYBODY get a bad NAME for that, |
| X | | and AS you say. |
| X | | that's what makes it AMERICA. |
| → X′ | Leo: | yeah |
| Y | | but it IS a shame. |
| Y | | and it uh UNFORTUNATELY: uh::, |
| Y | | (.) the fact that there are more people |
| | | like YOU marie, |
| Y | | than the REST, |
| Y | | (0.6) than the BA:D apples uh, |
| Y | | (.) kind of gets LOST in all of this. |

(Couper-Kuhlen and Thomson 2000: 388-389)

In (44), Marie expresses her thought that what at least some of the participants in the demonstration wanted to do was to make their opinion known. She was concerned about whether their sincere opinion was disparaged because the bombing had started too early, before efforts at negotiation had been exhausted. In line 8, she refers to earlier remark by the moderator that freedom of expression is a fundamental American right as far as it is peaceful. Then, the moderator Leo initially agrees with her saying *yeah* in line 10, but continue to evaluate what happened as a shame in line 11. His assessment is potentially incompatible with the positive aspect in which the basic right to freedom of expression has been presented.

However, the Cardinal Concessive schema allows him to claim that both points hold (Couper-Kuhlen and Thomson 2000: 389).

The example (44) shows that the X′ move can be realized by the single word *yeah.* The following example (45) shows more substantial conceding move. In the first turn of this extract, Mrs. Etchalls is in favor of prison: electronic bleepers are visible signs of one's conviction; *whoever you see... they know you've done something* in lines 2-3, and she says *a lot of people could just think you've gone on a holiday or something like that* in lines 5-6. This antithesis signifies the claim that prison is better. In line 7, Dick Hatch concedes both of Mrs. Etchalls' points by saying *I suppose they could.* In lines 8-11, he acknowledges that bleepers would be visible and make special countermeasures needed to solve the problem. However, in line 12, Mrs. Etchalls acknowledges his concession as Dick Hatch counters her claims (Y): *but...I think I would rather that than go to prison* (lines 14-16) (Couper-Kuhlen and Thomson 2000: 390).

(45) On this call to a British radio phone-in program, Mrs. Etchalls and the moderator Dick Hatch are comparing the advantages and disadvantages of a penal system in which people who are convicted of felonies wear electronic bleepers rather than go to prison.

| | | | |
|---|---|---|---|
| 1 | X | Etchalls: | everybody KNOWS |
| | X | | whoever you SEE don't they, |
| | X | | they know you've done SOMETHING, |

| | | |
|---|---|---|
| X | | whereas (0.7) YOU know, |
| X | | once you're-you're going (all) away. |
| X | | a lot of people could just think you've |
| X | | gone on a HOLIDAY or something li:ke tha:t. |
| X′ | Hatch | (0.4) I suppose they COULD, |
| X′ | | YES, I suppose it would mean that |
| X′ | | you'd have to spend quite a lot of time INDOORS, |
| X′ | | or else you'd have to wear a large MUFFLER all the time. |
| X′ | | or pretend you had a stiff NECK |
| X′ | | and wear one of those big PINK things they give you |
| | Etchalls: | (0.2) yeah |
| X′ | Hatch: | or something like THAT |
| Y | | (0.6) but I must say I THINK |
| Y | | It's the one sort of opinion I HAVE on the matter. |
| Y | | I think I would rather THAT than go to prison |
| | | because (0.2) PRISON must be VERY soul destroying. don't you think. |

(Couper-Kuhlen and Thomson 2000: 389-390)

This example above shows that, as indicated by the Xs, X′s and

Ys, the constituent parts of the Cardinal Concessive schema can be quite lengthy. Thus, the lexico-syntactic shape of the Concessive schema can be reduced or expanded depending on local contingencies in the interaction. The usage of Xs, X′s and Ys in the Cardinal Concessive template allows us to understand the wide divergence of lexico-syntactic forms (Couper-Kuhlen and Thomson 2000: 390).

As the second benefit of the Cardinal Concessive schema, it does not specify how the two parts X′ and Y are joined to one another, and this allows for various links. For instance, in example (42), Steve juxtaposes the two claims *outside of the Village they are (so characterless)* and *there's some in the Village that are nice,* but X′ and Y are linked by a parallelism between the two prepositional phrases and contrastive stress on *in* in the second one. In other words, the relation between X's and Ys may not be marked by any morphological markers at all (Couper-Kuhlen and Thomson 2000: 390).

In (44), speakers may connect Y to X′ with the coordinating conjunction *but.* In addition, the example (46) shows that speakers may also employ subordinating conjunctions in constructing Concessive patterns (Couper-Kuhlen and Thomson 2000: 391).

(46) Mr. Butler has called in to this Radio Manchester phone-in program to take exception to the point which an earlier caller, Mrs. Sack, made, namely that contaminated meats should not be used in the production of pet food. He refers here to dogs.

Butler: and I just WONDER
(0.2) WHY we SHOULD worry TOO much about what we put in their FOOD.
(0.6) er if-if-when you-
as soon as you let them off the LEAD.
or as soon as we SEE people LET them off a LEAD,
they immediately go SNIFFING ROUND.
(0.5) picking up all and sundry from the GROUND.
X and I just wonder what's the point in worrying
X about what goes in the TIN.
(1.2)
X′ Hatch well YES,
→ Y except that I mean you- you HAVE to RECOGNISE
Y as er (.) Mrs Sack said,
Y that there ARE a GREAT many PEOPLE,
Y who-whose LIVES are:
Y BUILT ROUND (.) to some extent,
Y (0.4) their-their PETS.

(Couper-Kuhlen and Thomson 2000: 391)

Mr. Butler expresses his point in a form of a rhetorical question such as *I just wonder what's the point in worrying about goes in the tin* in lines 8-9, which basically means that there is no point in worrying.... After a noticeable pause of 1.2 seconds, Dick Hatch initially agrees with what Mr. Butler has just said by saying *well yes* in line 10. However, he confronts with this point: *you have to recognize... that there are a gret many people... whose lives are built round... their pets* (lines 13-16). This remark implies that owners can be worried about the well-being of their pets. Worth noticing that Dick Hatch's counter-point Y is connected with his prior X's by the subordinator *except that* in line 11 (Couper-Kuhlen and Thomson 2000: 391-392).

Thus, there are a variety of means of explicitly linking X's and Y, and the Cardinal Concessive schema justifies this fact by under-specifying how its constitutive parts are conjoined. These advantages of the Cardinal Concessive allow us to understand better that acknowledging a previous speaker's point to be partially right and then making one's own contrasting point is a recurrent format with which speakers counter each others' claims (Couper-Kuhlen and Thomson 2000: 392).

## 3.2 Variations on the Cardinal Concessive

The Cardinal Concessive is characterized by the explicit presence of all three steps X, X′, Y and their presence in the order X, X′, Y. However, there are variations on the schema involving either the absence of one of the parts or a change in the order of the parts or both. Example (47) shows that speaker B does not first concede the validity of an interlocutor's point and then counters it, but in the next turn, speaker B makes a potentially incompatible point or claim and then he or she only subsequently acknowledges that speaker A's prior point was partially valid (Couper-Kuhlen and Thomson 2000: 392).

(47) Prior to this excerpt Charles has talked about a French friend Didier, who he describes as 'a musician and kind of cabaret artist.' The conversation then shifts to an occasion on which Charles heard Didier play some of his own songs and to another occasion on which Karen, a present co-participant, heard Didier's manager Ray sing. The topic of talk now reverts to Didier.

X  Steve: We'll I-dz--this guy's a CABARET artist,
I mean -
does [he PERFORM in
Y  Charles: [well I- I don't think he does that PROFESSIONAL-
X′  I mean he does-
X′  he: -he's had like a couple of en[gagements,
[oh Ray's his MANAGER.
Karen:
Charles: (--) HAN
Karen: I forgot,
right.
Charles: o:h MAN

Karen: and they-he just had a gig at (---)

STARBUCKS

(-) on the EAST side.

(Couper-Kuhlen and Thomson 2000: 393)

In line 1 above, Steve is asking Charles more about Didier's professional status. Steve repeats an earlier comment by Charles that *Didier is a cabaret artist.* Steve employs this earlier claim of Charles as background to his question in line 3 *does he perform in* ... In line 4, Charles introduces his counter-claim Y to correct the misinterpretation: *I don't think he does that professional.* This remark by Charles suggests that Steve's assumption was wrong. Worth noticing that Charles aborts his turn by producing the word *professionally* with a sound cut-off, and moreover, he weakens his prior counter-statement by saying that *Didier does* (line 5). Even though this turn is ruined, the contrastive stress on *does* implies that the label of 'cabaret artist' may be justified. Charles adds that Didier has had a couple of engagements (line 7), which means that "he is at least semi-professional." Therefore, lines 5-7 should be labeled as X′. Thus, the Contrastive Concessive allows for first a denial or contradiction (Y) of a prior statement and then an acknowledgement that his statement may partially right after all (X′) (Couper-Kuhlen and Thomson 2000: 393-394).

However, speakers often explicitly frame their talk in such a way that their conceding move is not the prominent part of their turn. There are some strategies that speakers can use to compensate for the natural prominence of X′ in end position. One strategy is for speaker B to repeat Y after producing X′ as shown in (48) (Couper-Kuhlen and Thomson 2000: 394).

(48) Two friends Ann and Barb are talking here about a mutual friend of theirs who has become seriously ill and given up on life. Brb has just asked rhetorically "What about the people who care about her and the people who are around?"

| | | |
|---|---|---|
| X | Ann: | she DOESN"T HAVE many people around her anymore. |
| Y | Barb: | but she DOES. |
| Y | | she DOES still have a lot of people who CARE |
| X′ | | (0.3) she doesn′t have anybody she′ll let get CLOSE to her, |
| → Y | | but he′s got a LOT of people who care. |
| | | (.hh) and a LO:T of people (.h) |
| | | you know the I:RMGARD Trassbachs, |
| | | (0.7) an-and (.h) CHRISTI: NE, |
| | | and CASS: |
| | | and people ALSO |
| | | who′ve never been CLOSE friends of hers, |
| | | (0.3) but who′d BEND over backwards (0.2) |
| | | for this woman. |

(Couper-Kuhlen and Thomson 2000: 394-395)

Ann argues that their friend *doesn't have any people around her anymore* as in line 1, and then Barb confronts this with Y i.e. *but she does* in their next turn as in line 2. Next Barb does her counter-claim with another Y *she does still have a lot of people who care* (line 3). This frame re-specifies the predicate as *having people around her who care.* Yet Barb continues to concede with an X′, *she doesn't have anybody she'll let get close to her* as in line 4. This acknowledgement plays a role of weakening the force of the prior contradictory move by suggesting that the interlocutor' s statement was partially right. However, Barb now reiterates her initial counterclaim (Y): *but she's got a lot of people who care* (line 5). Barb continues to introduce a list of people who care, and highlights the validity of her counterclaim. Thus, Barb does first disagreeing, and then retracting somewhat by weakly partially agreeing. In this variation where speaker B's conceding move (X′) follows the contrasting claim (Y), we often have sense that speaker B is 'backing down.' (Couper-Kuhlen and Thomson 2000: 395)

A second way to avoid the sequential implicativeness of an X′ in end position can be to disvalue it lexically and prosodically. This downplay is frequently done by deploying the unstressed particle *though* to represent X′ as seen in (49) (Couper-Kuhlen and Thomson 2000: 395).

(49) in this excerpt Lura has been talking about the frequent backaches. Ruth has reported her doctor's claim that everybody gets backaches because the backbone is 'built for an animal to walk on all fours'.

| | | |
|---|---|---|
| | Mom: | ACTUALLY |
| X | | that HELPS |
| X | | (-) when you have a backache. |
| | Laura: | really? |
| X | Mom: | (--) is to - |
| X | | (-) to get down on your hands and KNEES, |
| X | | and walk AROU- |
| | | and crawl AROUND |
| | Laura: | oh, |
| Y | | not crou- |
| Y, X′ | | not All the way DOWN though, |
| | Mom: | unh |

(Couper-Kuhlen and Thomson 2000: 395-396)

In (49), Mom provides X stating that backaches can be helped if you *get down on your hands and knees and ...crawl around* as in lines 2-8. Laura confronts this immediately with a Y, *oh, not crou... not all the way down* as in lines 9-11. She asserts that Mom's claim is not true, suggesting the possibility of a contrast between 'all the way down' and 'part way down.' Then, Laura appends the particle *though*, a way of acknowledging the partial validity of Mom's prior statement. According to Pomerantz, a final particle *though* serves as "claiming to agree with the prior while marking, and accompanying, a shift in assessed parameters which partially contrasts with the prior" (1984: 63). This is indicated with the notation Y X′ in line 11. Laura's conceding move is lexico-syntactically and prosodically reduced, and *though* does not form a separate intonation phrase but instead is attached to the prior intonation phrase. In this case the intonation phrase consists of the entirety of Y, where it is in post-tonic position. Hence, X′ is scarcely imported but Y remains prominent although it is not in end position. Thus, example (49) implies that in subsequent talk the speakers do not focus on how getting down on all fours helps a backache (X), but highlight how going down all the way is not helpful (Y). For instance, mom produces a negative agreement token in line 12 (Couper-Kuhlen and Thomson 2000: 396).

In sum, a variation on the Cardinal Concessive Schema is the X Y X′ pattern. In other words, when one speaker provides claims (X), he or she presents their counterclaim (Y) first, and then acknowledge that all or part of the previous speaker's claim has some validity (X′) (Couper-Kuhlen and Thomson 2000: 396).

The second type of variation is the pattern [X, X′], without Y. That Y is missing is surprising, given the previous claim that the third move is the thrust of speaker B's turn. Example (50) shows that speakers actually refrain from producing a projected Y by appealing to a tacit understanding of it (Couper-Kuhlen and Thomson 2000: 397):

(50) Harold, Miles, Pete and Jamie are gossiping about a neighbor who has recently produced a number of 'brat' kids.

| 1 | X | Harold: | does she even have a b- a MAN? |
|---|---|---|---|
| | X | | I guess she MUST. |
| | | Miles: | (0.5) does she have a WHAT? |

Jamie: [a MA.N.
Harold: [a MA.N.
Pete: (.hh)
X′ Jamie: she has SOME [kind of a-
X′ Miles: [at least TEMPORSRILY,
Pete: [yeah,
Harold: [yeah.
Jamie: heh heh (.h) [at ONE time
X′ Harold: [for about FIVE minutes,
X′ PROBABLY.
Miles: heh
Pete: heh

(Couper-Kuhlen and Thomson 2000: 397)

At the beginning of conversation, in (50), Harold asks a question such as *Does she even have a man*? as in line 1, which he then proceeds to answer himself such as *I guess she must* in line 2. This made the point 'She must have a man', which we are calling X. After a short repair sequence in lines 3-5, Jamie and Miles concede their positions about this point in partial overlap by putting strong stress 'some' in Jamie's *she has some kind of a-,* in line 7 and on *temporarily* in Miles' *at least temporarily* in line 8 (Couper-Kuhlen and Thomson 2000: 397).

Here, Jamie and Miles each partition Harold's claim X in a different way. In Jamie's *she has some kind of a-* the stress on *some* makes it possible to contrast 'some kind of man' with 'the real kind of man.' Stressing on *temporarily* in Miles' *at least temporarily* (line 8) sets up a contrast between 'temporarily' vs. 'permanently.' In each case, these contrastive stresses on the first part of the contrast allow for projecting the second part. Notice that in each case the counter-move Y (i.e. *but she doesn't have the real thing or but she doesn't have one permanently*) is missing. The projectability of these counter-moves (Ys) serves as a base for enjoyment which Janie, Miles and Pete share in lines 11 and 14-15 (Couper-Kuhlen and Thomson 2000: 397-398).

Thus, the second variation on the Cardinal Concessive is that the third move, speaker B's counter-claim, called Y, is missing. Y can be omitted in all such cases of concession, if it is strongly projected by the first two moves, X and X′. Worth noticing that as shown in (50), this second variation is accomplished with two common strategies such as prosody and partitioning (Couper-Kuhlen and Thomson 2000: 398).

### 3.3 Functional considerations

Concession in English conversation can be understood in terms of a Cardinal Schema according to which they partially acknowledge another's point (X′), and then make their own potentially incompatible point (Y). The patterns apply to dyadic interaction, and they are not random nor coincidental formations. Rather, the dyadic patterns seem to have grown out of tasks which participants find themselves continually confronted with in interaction. The Cardinal Concessive well represents prefacing a disagreeing move with partial or weak agreement in the context of an assessing activity. Prefacing disagreement with an initial agreement is a way of negotiating alignment with one another in interaction (Pomerantz 1984). Example (42), which is about the coffeehouses located *inside* and *outside* the Village, demonstrates well the strategic use to which the Cardinal Concessive together with partitioning can be put (Couper-Kuhlen and Thomson 2000: 402-403).

Disagreement-prefacing is particularly associated with the use of the Cardinal Concessive schema in an argumentative context. Here the conceding move X′, *bleepers* has a decidedly rhetorical effect. In other words, one makes one's own counter-claim formidable by setting up an opponent's case strongly. Speakers need not pursue alignment in an argumentative context, and as shown in example (45), interlocutors do not reach consensus on whether beepers or prison is better for felons. However, example (51) shows that Cardinal Concessives are employed not only in disalignment contexts but also in alignment contexts (Couper-Kuhlen and Thomson 2000: 403).

(51) Connie, Vera and her boyfriend Ketih are talking about Vera's father, who is suffering from the aftermath of a knee operation. In prior conversation it has emerged that Vera's mother has led her to question whether the operation was necessary in the first place. Just prior to this excerpt Connie has pointed out that Vera's father was in considerable pain before the operation.

Kei: How come (0.2) you're letting this
CRA[ZY person change your mind,
Ver: [right.
Kei: you [know.
Ver: [well s- it's like she made me
believe that,
YEAH,
you know the doctors ARE (.) you know
horrible,
and yes this is ridiculous,
an. hh gu- I gue [ss-
Con: [why do you think your-
X mom is probably just-
X Ver: JEALOUS.
Kei: eh h[eh
X′ Con: [well I mean pr- maybe that too,
Y but she just can't HANDLE (0.2) [people
close to her being in PAIN.
Ver: [reality.

(Couper-Kuhlen and Thomson 2000: 403-404)

In line 9, Connie questions Vera's assessment of their mother's behavior such as *why do you think your-*. *Your* plays a pivotal role in Connie's next turn, which introduces an alternative explanation for Vera's mom's behavior, i.e. *(your) mom is probably just-* in line 10. This partially complete turn is completed by Vera with *jealous* in line 11. In accordance with Cardinal Concessives, the utterance such as *Mom is probably just jealous* can be labeled X. In her next turn, Connie acknowledges that *this may be true well I mean ... maybe that two* in line 13, which can be labeled X′. In this case, Connie's counter-claim Y, is being presented by Connie as compatible while potentially incompatible with Vera's claim X. Thus, example (51) shows that Concession may be employed as an alignment strategy as readily as a disalignment strategy (Couper-Kuhlen and Thomson 2000: 404).

The variation, in which the counter-claim Y is followed by conceding move X′, is labeled as [X Y X′]. In this variation, speaker B makes a contradiction or denial followed by modifying or weakening it subsequently. When the X′ move remains in end position, and has implications for subsequent talk, speaker B will often form a claim which is found to be too strong. The concessive pattern, [X Y X′] functions as a means of self-correction (Couper-Kuhlen and Thomson 2000: 404).

However, [X Y X′] variations with X′ realized as *though* are adapted to quite different environments. In this variation, since the conceding move is so strongly backgrounded, Y move, which is the contradiction or denial, goes on a record. As shown in (50), however, it can be weakened if partitioning is employed. Also note that Laura' *not all the way* in (49) is more softened way of disagreeing with the statement *that helps when you have a backache... is to get down your hands and knees and... crawl around* than would be 'no it doesn't.' Likewise, this move may leave some room for the other to be partially right (Couper-Kuhlen and Thomson 2000: 404-405).

## 3.4 Concessive *but*-constructions in Spoken Discourse

Previous studies have claimed that concessive relations are rare in spoken language (Di Meola 1997: 10, Hermodsson 1978: 65). This claim has been supported by the results of a number of quantitative studies (Ford 1993; Stojanova-Jovceva 1979; Brunet 1995). Ford (1993) identifies only 3 concessive of the 197 adverbial constructions in her corpus, which can be explained by the complexity of concessive constructions. In addition, König (1988) also proposes that "[a]n elaborate inventory of concessive expressions... presupposes, it seems, a certain tradition of argumentative writing." (Barth 1988: 145; 2000: 411)

Kauffmann (1974) suggests, through an analysis of a corpus of spoken English, that speakers also can concede their interlocutor' s point, though their means may be different from those of writers (Kauffmann 1974: 2). But there have been not many studies on these means in spoken discourse and moreover, most of the studies have been limited to ideal sentences (e.g., König 1994; Lotscher 1988). Even when real, not ideal, examples are investigated, they are usually taken from written discourses (e.g., Di Meola 1997; Rudoplh 1996; Ford 1993; Barth 2000: 412).

Thus, concessive relations in spoken discourse have, for the most part, not attracted attention (cf. Di Meola's claim) and have not been considered significant. In this section, we will take a close look at two concessive constructions *but* and *although* focusing on their discourse functions and the constructions' specific way of realizing the concessive schema (Barth 2000: 412). Couper-Kuhlen and Thompson (1999), drawing on Rhetorical Structure Theory (e.g., Schegloff, Jefferson and Sacks 1977; Pomerantz 1984; Sacks 1987), points to the inherently interactive nature of concessivity: one speaker acknowledges a claim made by another, and allows him or her to disagree in a mitigated way. As discussed in the previous section, the Cardinal Concessive schema depicts an idealized situation where a speaker makes some statement (X), whereupon another speaker acknowledges that this may be partially right (X′) but claims that something can be incompatible (Y). More schematically this looks as follows in (52) (Barth 2000: 413):

(52)

A: X (stating something or making some point)

B: X′ (acknowledging the validity of this statement or point, the conceding move)

Y (claiming the validity of a potentially contrasting statement or point)

(Barth 2000: 413)

As explained in the previous section, the Cardinal Concessive schema is not the only way to accomplish concession, but there can be variation with respect to the sequence of the elements of the concessive schema, the number of participants involved in producing the concessive schema, and variation in countermarking. Barth

(2000) has investigated 8.5 hours of mainly spontaneous spoken, public and private British and American English data throughly for all realizations of the concessive relation (Barth 2000: 414).

One variation where the sequence of X′ and Y is reversed includes about 34% of the examples in the corpus. Example (53) illustrates such a case(Barth 2000: 414):

(53) Presidential debate: Jim Baker (20.01; 55:12)

(American English public TV discussion; second part of the presidential debate between Bush, Clinton, and Perot, in which journalists ask the candidates questions. Susan Ross is pointing to the small number of women and ethnic minorities I key positions in Bush's government)

X Sus: .hh but whE:n we lOO:k;
at the cIrcle of the kEY: pEople clOsest to you; (.)
your Inner cIrcle of adVIsors;
wE see whIte mEn Only. (.)
whY:?
and whEn will that chAnge.

(Barth 2000: 414)

[23lines omitted in which Bush defend himself by listing women hold influential positions in his government]

Y Bush: you can lOOK all arOUnd,
and you'll see first clAss strOng WOmen;

X′ uh: (.) jim bAker's a mA:n. (.)
yeah I agrE=i plead gUIlty to that;
Y′ but lOOK arOUnd who's/- (.)
lOOk who's arOUnd wIth him there
i mean thIs is a little defENsive on your part.

(Barth 2000: 414-415)

In this example, the counterclaim (Y) is followed by conceding move (X′). Sue makes a claim that Bush discriminate against women and ethnic minorities (X), and then Bush defends himself against this accusation (Y), followed by ironically acknowledging that part of the accusation is true. The concessive pattern is as follows in (54) (Barth 2000: 415):

(54)

X Sus: why do you discriminate against women and ethnic minorities in key positions
Y Bush: I don't, look at the women I have in my staff
X′ yes, there is a white man, Jim Baker
Y′ but there are so many women that he hardly counts

(Barth 2000: 415)

There is also a variation in number of participants involved in producing the concessive schema. Although the Cardinal Concessive schema is dialogic, in monologic variants one speaker may produce a concessive relation. Pseudo-dyadic and monadic variations can be distinguished: In the pseudo-dyadic variation, the speaker produces an entire Cardinal Concessive on his or her own, fulfilling the roles of both A and B, as shown in (55) (Barth 2000: 415).

(55) Presidential debate: Incumbent (20.01; 1:23:32)

(American English public TV discussion; first part of the presidential debate between Bush, Clinton and Perot, in which the candidates react to questions posed by the moderator. Here Bush is defending himself as the current incumbent against governor Clinton's attacks by accusing Clinton himself.)

| | | |
|---|---|---|
| | Bush: | hE keeps criticizing Us. |
| | | criticizing mE. |
| X | | I'm the incUmbent. |
| X′ | | fine. |
| Y | | but HE's an incumbent. |
| | | and we've got to look at All the facts; |

(Barth 2000: 415-416)

In (55), as Bush points to Clinton's criticism of himself in line 2, he says that he (=Bush) is the incumbent (X) in line 3. This statement was made to imply that Bush was not a successful President. Bush partially concedes Clinton's argument by saying *fine* (X′) in line 4 and then confronts it by referring to Clinton's status. In addition, Bush puts stress on *he* in *He's an incumbent* (Y) in line 5. Worth noticing that all three parts of the concessive schema are realized by one single speaker, Bush. This variation amounts to only about 2% of all the relevant examples in the corpus. On the other hand, monadic variations, with 36%, are quite frequent in the corpus. As illustrated in (56), the speaker speculates the existence of some previous X, and then concedes it implicitly (Barth 2000: 416).

(56) Don Vogel: Flashy (8.02; 55:14)

(American English radio show, Don VOgel and T.D. Mishky are broadcasting from the Minnesota state fair. T.D. has asked Don, who is blind, how he manages to dress well-matched. Don has answered that he only buys matching clothes so that he cannot make wrong choices.)

TD: there's a lEsson in that for All of us.
Don: uh hm. (.)
yEAh it's very EAsy.
X′ now you cAn' dress rEAl FLASHy. (.)
by dOing it that wAY;
Y bU:t (.) you know i'd rAther be (.) able to sort of mA:tch;
than to be real flAshy.
[you kn()w what I mean?
TD: [uh hm,
Don: so: -(.)

(Barth 2000: 416)

As T.D. praised Don's method of buying clothes in line 1, Don reacts to this compliment by making his own merit not serious in lines 2-3 (Pomerantz 1984). He keeps acknowledging a possible disadvantage to an 'otherwise extremely advisable practice': *you can't dress real flashy by doing it that way* (X′) in lines 4-5, which means that in fact it is not such a good practice. However, he dismisses this possible counterclaim by downplaying his ability to dress flashy: I'd rather be able to sort of match in lines 6-9 (Barth 2000: 416-417).

Worth noticing that none of the examples given so far represent concessive relation marked by *although* or *even though*. Instead, it is marked by *but*. Table 7 presents a frequency list for marking concessive relations in the corpus of spoken data, and in written data, taken from Rudolph (1996) (Barth 2000: 417).

Table 7. Frequency list of realization of concessive relations in spoken and written English (Barth 2000: 417)

| Spoken data (in 8.5 hours)(total:317) | Written data(adapted from Rudolph 1996: 5) |
|---|---|
| 260 *but*-constructions | *though* |
| 36 asyndetic constructions | *although* |
| 6 *and*-construction | *in spite of* |
| (of all these:19 with final *though* | *despite* |
| 3 with...*though*...) | *even though* |
| 4 *on the other hand*-constructions | *even when* |
| 3 *and yet*-construction | *...though...* |
| 2 *although*-constructions | *although-in fact* |
| 1 initial *though*-construction | *although-nevertheless* |
| 1 yet-construction | *though-all the same* |
| 1 *nevertheless*-construction | *even if* |
| 1 *while*-construction | *albeit* |
| 1 *apart from* that-construction | *...as....* |
| 1 *or*-construction | *...that...* |

The number of concessive relations found in this spoken corpus clearly shows that concession is not infrequent in spoken language. Note that markers such as *on the other hand* traditionally categorized as 'adversative' (e.g. Rudolph 1996: 4; Quirk et al. 1985: 635-636), are included as concessive in the corpus (Barth 2000: 417-418).

Table 7 shows that the items at the top of the two lists are considerably different: while *though* and *although* are frequently used in written concessive relations, they are not frequent in spoken discourse, except for final *though.* Conjunction *but* is the top item on the list of spoken concessive relations, but it is not included by Rudolph at all (Barth 2000: 418).

There is no need to account for the overwhelming predominance of *but*-constructions in expressing concessivity in speaking. The observed distribution of concessive constructions in spoken discourse as compared to written discourse can be explained by the advantage of coordinating constructions such as *but.* Spoken language is often demanding for both speaker and hearer because a large amount of data is produced and processed within a short period of time. Therefore, the speakers or hearers can not return to 'difficult stretches of text' in order to process them if they interrupt the flow of discourse. The speakers often avoid cognitively more demanding subordinate structures and employ coordinating constructions, for paratactic relations can simplify this high speed on-line language production and processing (e.g. Chafe 1988; Ochs 1979; but e.g. Beaman 1984; Barth 2000: 417).

Another advantage of coordinate constructions such as *but* is that the constructions can balance the weight of the connected propositions while hypotactic constructions subordinate the opposing argument (Grote, Lenke, and Stede 1997). Paratactic concessive constructions lend some weight to this argument X at first, and then contrast it with Y. Therefore, the speaker can preserve a certain amount of room to negotiate, which makes it possible that the propositions still have an equal chance to be valid. At the end of this negotiation, it becomes clear which of the arguments is dominated or subordinated. Nevertheless, using coordinating structures makes it possible to change sides without losing too much face when interlocutors suddenly adopt an opposing point of view (Mulkay 1985; Barth 2000: 419).

Thus, concessive *but*-constructions have the strategy of granting equal weight to both propositions, and therby have an advantage for namely the possibility of saving not only the speaker's own face but also that of her interlocutor. While hypotactic constructions subordinate the opposing argument (Y) and thereby can make the face-threatening argument, paratactic constructions allow the speaker to include the conceding part needed to save the counterpart's face. Thus, concessive *but*-constructions employ various means such as explicit first agreement (X′) to delay the dispreferred move (Pomerantz 1984). This delay allows the first speaker to reformulate the point on which her conversational partner disagrees (Koerfer 1979; Barth 2000: 419).

Thus, coordinating constructions are useful means for the realization of concessive relations in spoken language. This is reflected in their high frequency of concessive *but* and in turn low frequency of *although*-constructions in spoken discourse (Barth 2000: 420).

## 3.5 Discourse Functions of *although*-constructions in Spoken language

A data of spontaneously produced concessive *but*-and *although*-constructions was compiled from the 8.5 hour corpus and the number of concessive *although* constructions was extended by further investigation of 50 hours of spoken English data, as shown in Table 8 (Barth 2000: 420).

Table 8. Examples included in the further investigation

| construction | Number of examples |
|---|---|
| concessive *although*-constructions | 26 |
| concessive *but*-constructions | 260 |

(Barth 2000: 420)

The concessive *although*-constructions have at least four functions: i) restricting previous claims; ii) introducing additional information; iii) forestalling possible objections; iv) summarizing the previous exchange of arguments. These functions mostly have a discourse-organizational nature. These functions occur in overlap, either with the conceding function or partly with each other. Therefore, the percentages in Table 9, which illustrates the frequency of these functions, exceed 100%. as shown below (Barth 2000: 420)

Table 9. Frequency of discourse functions of concessive *although*-constructions

| Function | Number of examples (total: 26) |
|---|---|
| Restricting previous claims | 19(73%) |
| Introducing additional information | 15(58%) |
| Forestalling a possible objection | 13(50%) |
| Summarizing a previous exchange of arguments | 3(12%) |
| Insertion | 14(56%) |
| Topic shift | 4(16%) |

(Barth 2000: 421)

### 3.5.1 Restricting previous claims

As shown in Table 9, the most frequent function of concessive *although*-constructions in spoken discourse is to restrict previous claims. Restricting constructions are characterized by a second proposition which limits the validity of the previous claim, as is illustrated in (57) (Barth 2000: 421):

(57) Colin Blakemore: Ulcer (24.04; 1: 03:50)

(British English radio programme. Antony Clair is interviewing Professor Colin Blakemore, a well-known neurologist. Clair has been trying to pinpoint reasons for Blakemore's success, one of which he assumes to be Blakemore's having suffered from a gastric ulcer in his youth, which could have been fatal.)

Clair: .hh so there's a sense of lIving what on
borrowed tIme even;
that this is tIme you hadn't expEcted;
you pAck it full;
you nEver know when the/-
=although in fact that partIcular problem was EAsed as uh
the ULcer,
and the blEEding,
[and/
Blake: [i hAd an operAtion when itwEnty; uh gastrActomy,

(Barth 2000: 421)

In lines 1-5, after Clair stated that Blakmore is now living on borrowed time, giving him motivation to fulfill his job so successfully, he realized that his claim is slightly overstated. In lines 6-9, Claire downplays his claim by pointing to a fact, i.e. *that particular problem was eased.* He thus restricts the validity of X, i.e. Blakemore's suffering is the reason for his success in his career today (Barth 2000: 422).

This example seems to represent a correction at first sight, but it is in fact still restrictive: Clair does not make a claim that Blackmore has not had any problem, but he only refers to an improvements in Blakemore's situations. In contrast to a correction, where the validity of the previous claim is canceled and which may therefore not be considered concessive, in the case of restriction, it is still valid. Restricting the validity of the previous claim is a strategy often employed when the speaker expects an unfavourable response, such as disagreement (Pomerantz 1984; Barth 2000: 422).

### 3.5.2 Introducing additional information

The function of introducing additional information is also closely related to the restrictive function of *although*-clauses. This close relationship is reflected in the fact that additional information often restricts the validity of the previous claim. In (57), Clair' s information that Blackmore's suffering was over at a particular point downplays his earlier overstatement. Another example is as follows in (58) (Barth 2000: 422-423):

(58) Larry Bensky: Common Cause (71.01; 51:42)

(American English radio show, Larry Bensky, the host, is interviewing Ann McBride, director of Common Cause, an American grass-roots movement for making politics more efficient. They are talking about support for their goals by politicians, such as the Republican congressman Shace. He, when interviewer the week before, admitted that with the present reform measure they only achieved a compromise.)

Larry: he bAsically said;
... [2 lines reported speech omitted]
it's nOt even very gOOd;
but it's All we can get thrOUgh there;
X [=thAt's]=not=really gOOd enough

X′ Ann: [well]
well It is nO:t good enough as it is right NOW;
X′a althOUgh in the last wEEk,
uh our understAnding is,
that they have wOrked to strEngthen their lObby/ (.)
lObbyist gIft ban, (.)
Y hhh but hE is at lEAst talking about
pUtting these Issues on the TA:ble;
and i'll tEll you whAt;
X Larry: the reform measure you got through is not really good enough
X′ Ann: well, it is not good enough as it is right now
X′a although we heard that they have worked on strengthening
the lobbyist gift ban
Y but he is at least putting these issues on the table

(Barth 2000: 423)

In line 7-9, Ann partly agrees with Larry's criticism that the present reform measure is not good enough. The stress on *now* implies that the reform measure can be better at some other point in time. Then She highlights that the situation is actually not as bad as her previous claim suggests, since they have succeeded partially in working on a lobbyist gift ban in lines 10-13. The information is less directly associated with the line of argumentation because it gives additional background information, whose validity in the present context is signified by *although*. At the same time the information limits the validity of X′ and thus in a way already indicates an upcoming opposing Y. Then, Ann returns to the original concessive *but*-construction and ends it in lines 14-15 (Barth 2000: 423-424).

### 3.5.3 Forestalling a possible objection

Forestalling a possible opposition is the third frequent function of concessive *although*-constructions (also König, 1988: 148). Speakers expect counterclaims to their statement and they may 'invalidate' them in their own turn before their counterpart has a chance to object to it as shown in (59) (Barth 2000: 424).

(59) Bernie Hermann: The rising sun (44.01; 49:35)

(American English radio-phone-in show with Bernie Hermann on the dropping of the Hiroshima bomb. Bernie is defending it by referring to the war situation at that time; he agrees with the previous caller, who has also pointed out that there was a anger of Russia possibly invading Japan.)

Bern: although the russians dId declare war on Japan very very lAte
a:nd they dId go into manchUria;
Y but/h we were concErned,(.)
about their getting tOO strong a fOOthold in Asia
and perhAps; (.)
X′ uh although uh mister trUman never sAId that,
Y′ uh uh that might have been an (underlying)/
anOther one of the rEAsons, (.)

whY the bomb was drOpped.

(Barth 2000: 424)

In the example above, Bernie claims that the bomb may have been dropped because the United States was concerned about Russia's strong foothold in Asia (Y) as seen in lines 4-7 and in lines 9-12. However, he is aware of possible objection from other people because no one ever stated this as a possible reason for bombing. He acknowledges that 'this is not a reason given officially' by saying *Mister Truman never said that* (X′) in line 8, and thereby prevents such possible objection. The concessive schema of (59) is as follows in (60) (Barth 2000: 425):

(60)

| | | |
|---|---|---|
| Y | Bernie: | we were concerned about their getting a foothold in Asia and perhaps |
| X′ | | although mister truman never said that |
| Y | | that might have been another reason why the bomb was dropped |

(Barth 2000: 425)

Giving additional information also serves this function in that the additional information, which depicts the situation more accurately, could also be interpreted as forestalling a possible objection from the other interlocutor (Barth 2000: 425).

### 3.5.4 Summarizing a previous exchange of arguments

A fourth function of *although*-relation is that *although*-construction summarizes the points discussed in the preceding co-text, and accomplishes a more global discourse task, as illustrated in (61) (Barth 2000: 425):

(61) Any Questions: Bargain (47.01; 13:13)

(British English radio discussion in which the panel answers questions from the audience. Here they are discussing a proposed pay deal with the TGWU according to which its members would be given private medical treatment. After another panel member has criticized this proposal, Enoch Powell now takes a turn.)

X Pow: I suppose I stArt with a prEjudice in favour of thOse who
are bArgaining,
arrIving at a bargain at the End of it,
which eh sUIts both pArties.
Y but uh I dOn't like,
pAY:,
in the form of (.) frInge bEnefits or bEnefits in kInd,
or Anything Other than straight wAges;
I think it Always ends/ lEAds in the end to trOUble,
...[4 lines elaborating on the trouble omitted]
Y uh so,
X' althOUgh (.) I wouldn't wish to interfEre with such a bargain, I wouldn't wish gOvernment or lEgislation to

interfere with such a gargain being arrived at,

Y I hOpe that sort of bargain is not going to become tYpical because...[5lines on the reason omitted] uh On the matter of uh (.) bUYing (.) cAre-

(Barth 2000: 425-426)

In the example above, Powell points out how hard it is to reach a bargain in remuneration negotiations in lines 1-4, and acknowledges that payment *in the form of...anything other than straight wages... always...*may cause a problem in lines 5-15. Powell has contrasted two propositions: X, 'promising some trade union members advantages is not to be criticised,' and Y, 'remuneration other than in straight ways leads to trouble and is to be criticized'. After the explanation of Y, he summarizes his point redundantly by packaging X and Y neatly in an *although*-construction. The concessive schema of example (61) looks as follows in (62) (Barth 2000: 426):

(62)

Y Powell: so

X′ although I wouldn't wish anyone to interfere with such a bargain(once it has been arrived at)
(implied: such bargains are to be valued, I.e. promising advantages is not to be criticized)

Y I hope such bargains are not going to become typical (implied: such bargains are to be criticized)

(Barth 2000: 426)

These summarizing *although*-constructions are similar to concessive relations in writing, but they are infrequent (12%) in spoken discourse as in Table 9. This is related to the fact that spoken language is usually employed to exchange or negotiate opinions about the state of the world, that is, the relationship between X and Y, but written language is deployed to report the result of this conversation or negotiation (Barth 2000: 426).

### 3.6 Concessive *although*- vs. *but*-constructions

Concessive *but*-constructions and *although*-ones have difference in the number of speakers. As shown in Table 10, while concessive *but*-constructions are mainly produced by more than one speaker, the majority of the concessive *although*-constructions is realized by one speaker. This is related to tasks such as giving additional information (in the case of (58)), preventing a possible opposition from an interlocutor (in the case of (59)) or summarizing the previous negotiation (in the case of (61)), because the tasks fulfilled by *although*-constructions are usually accomplished by one of the interlocutors (Barth 2000: 427).

In contrast to *although*-constructions, concessive *but*-constructions, in contrast, may be employed for tasks such as dealing with explicitly stated counter-arguments by other speakers or its dyadic variation and dealing with possible objections from an interlocutor. Likewise, the predominance of dialogic patterns with *but*-constructions can be reflected in Table 10, and be explained by the discourse origin of concessive *but*-constructions(Hopper 1987 on emergent grammar; König 1985a, 1985b; Barth 2000: 427).

Table 10. Number of speakers in concessive *but*- and *although*-constructions

| Number of speakers | ***but*** (total: 260) | ***although*** (total:26) |
|---|---|---|
| one | 122 (47%)*** | 22 (85%)*** |
| more than one | 138 (53%)*** | 4 (15%)*** |

(Barth 2000: 427)

In terms of the realization of the elements of the concessive schema, the two concessive constructions, *although*-constructions and *but*-constructions also differ. In concessive *but*-constructions, the argument of the fist speaker, called X, is predominantly made explicit as shown in Table 11. Table 11 shows that in concessive *although*-constructions, the argument X is not often expressed. This is also associated with the tasks such as giving additional information as well as preventing a possible objections, because the information and/or the objection are not usually made explicit, which means there is no X (Barth 2000: 428).

Table 11. Realization of X in concessive *but*- and *although*-constructions

| Realization of X | ***but*** (total: 260) | ***although*** (total:26) |
|---|---|---|
| not realized | 110 (42%) *** | 20 (77%) *** |
| realized | 150 (58%) *** | 6 (23%) *** |

(Barth 2000: 428)

As shown in Table 12, these tasks such as giving additional information and preventing possible objections also explain why concessive *although*-constructions frequently introduce a 'new' X′: in other words, X cannot be taken up with additional information and possible objections. In contrast, with the majority of the concessive *but*-constructions, speaker B takes up X in X′ (Barth 2000: 428).

Table 12. Realization of X′ in concessive *but*- and *although*-constructions

| Realization of X′ | ***but*** (total: 260) | ***although*** (total:26) |
|---|---|---|
| not realized | 110 (42%) *** | 20 (77%) *** |
| realized | 150 (58%) *** | 6 (23%) *** |

The most significant function of *although*-constructions, that is to say, restricting the validity of a previous claim is associated with one of the surface characteristics of this construction: "only those claims which have already been made can be restricted" (Barth 2000: 428). Hence, as *although*-constructions restrict the validity of the claim, X′ occur in post-position, which explains the predominance of postposed *although*-clauses as shown in Table 13 (Barth 2000: 428).

In concessive *but*-constructions, a preceding X occurs explicitly and X′ occurs mainly before Y. X′ is also inserted between Y and Y′, in order to forestall a possible objection or to acknowledge the validity of the preceding X after it has already been countered (Barth 2000: 429).

Table 13. Position of X′ with respect to Y in concessive *but*- and *although*- constructions

| Realization of X′ | ***but*** (total: 260) | ***although*** (total:26) |
|---|---|---|
| pre-position | 178(68%)*** | 1(4%)*** |
| post-position | 18( 7%)*** | 14(54%)*** |
| split position | 64 (25%)* | 11(42%)* |

(Barth 2000: 429)

Werlich(1976) distinguishes five text types: descriptive, narrative, expository, instructive, and argumentative, but a text can comprise more than one text type. For instance, even though the televised presidential debate can be described as argumentative, there are descriptive, narrative, and expository parts in it.

Table 14 shows that both *although*- and *but*- constructions prefer descriptive-expository environments but there are also significant differences with respect to their distribution over the text types. While concessive *but*-constructions also occur frequently in argumentative environments (König 1988), concessive *although*-constructions are not frequent in this context. Rather *although*-constructions occur more frequently in narrative-descriptive parts of texts. In addition, they occur a little more frequently in descriptive-expository contexts than *but*-constructions (Barth 2000: 429-430).

Table 14. Distribution of concessive *but*- and *although*- constructions according to text type

| Distribution according to text type | ***but*** (total:260) | ***although*** (total: 26) |
|---|---|---|
| descriptive-expository | 154 (59%)* | 20 (77%)* |
| instructive | 18 ( 7%) | 1 ( 4%) |
| narrative-descriptive | 19 ( 7%) | 4 (15%) |
| argumantative | 69 (27%)*** | 1 ( 4%)*** |

(Barth 2000: 430)

Thus, *although*-constructions occur frequently in contexts where the opinion about the state of affairs has already been decided upon. In that regard, *although*-constructions are more likely to occur in reporting text types such as descriptive-expository and narrative-descriptive text types than in argumentative ones. On the other hand, concessive *but*-constructions are frequent in argumentative contexts (Barth 2000: 430).

## 3.7 Concessive Patterns in Conversation

Students of discourse have long been interested in a recurrent set of morpho-syntactive patterns in which speakers are 'conceding' that addressees are or might be right about something that the speakers are taking issue with. Let us take a look at an example from our conversational database (Couper-Kuhlen and Thomson 2000: 381).

(63) Joanne and Leonore are discussing a mutual friend who has engaged in a substance abuse.

Joanne: but he's healthy as on OX,
that guy.
(---) (h) that guy is HEAL [ THY as an o:x.
a Leonore: [his liver,
a → except for his liver.
Joanne: (-) yeah,
but I'm saying,
is like
you know,
b → as much as he's ABU:SED his liver
and all other (-) other things in his life,
he's still HEALTHY as an OX.

(Couper-Kuhlen and Thomson 2000: 381)

If you take a look at lines 4 and 5, Leonore points out that their mutual friend's liver is not healthy. In line 10, Joanne acknowledges that there is something right about what Leonore has said, i.e. *his liver is not healthy*, but in line 12, she persists in her claim that *he is still healthy as an ox.* This example shows four recurrent features of patterns: first, 'conceding' is something in daily conversation that people do in conversing with each other. Acknowledging Leonore's claim makes it possible for Joanne to disagree in mitigated form. Pomerantz (1984) claims that conceding is a way of allowing speakers to carry out a potentially disruptive disagreement. As demonstrated in the example above, conceding involves a 3-part interactional sequence as in (64) (Couper-Kuhlen and

Thomson 2000: 382).

(64)

1st move A: States something or makes some point

2nd move B: Acknowledges the validity of this statement or point (the conceding move)

3rd move B: Goes onto claim the validity of a potentially contrasting statement or point

(Couper-Kuhlen and Thomson 2000: 382)

Conceding is essentially dyadic: it basically requires at least two parties, one who concedes and one to whom or for whom the concession is made. The speaker who concedes is doing so in order to make his/her own potentially contrasting point. In this regard, 'conceding' can be understood as one way in which speakers can select to express 'contrast' (Couper-Kuhlen and Thomson 2000: 382).

The way in which X and Y are understood by the participants as contrasting cannot be defined in advance, but can be interpreted and negotiated by the participants in the situated context. The notion of 'conceding' has interested linguists primarily in two aspects: First, concessive has been focused as a type of clause combination, and scholars have investigated concessive clauses in relation to their main clauses (especially König 1985a, 1985b, 1986, 1988, Altenberg 1986, Sweetser 1990, Karantzola 1995, Gunthner 1999); Second, concession has been studied in terms of a text relation (see e.g., Martin 1992; Mann and Thompson 1988, 1992; Thompson

1987; Matthiessen 1995; Rudolph 1996; Azar 1997; Reinhardt 1997; Couper-Kuhlen and Thomson 2000: 382-383).

In addition, Antako and Wetherell (1999) identify what they call 'show concession', a pattern not identical but related to the ones described here, in which speakers address some vulnerability in their starting claim and by making a show of conceding it, they achieve the rhetorical effect of fortifying their own position (Couper-Kuhlen and Thomson 2000: 383).

A number of concessive relations, although they have underlying three-part structures, are represented as two-part structures with either the presupposition or the implicit denial. Example (65) comprises a three-part structure of statement-denial-reason for denial. By making the denial in the second sentence in (65) implicit with a concessive construction, as shown in (66), the same information can be represented in a less marked way (Jordan 1998: 727).

(65) Is reducing salt the first thing you think about when you hear high blood pressure? It turns out that the diet-blood pressure link may *not* be quite so simple. An accumulation of research is showing that two little calcium, potassium and magnesium also plays an important role.

(*Maclean's*, March 20 1995: 5; extracted from Jordan 1998: 727)

(66) '*Although* reducing salt might be the first thing you think about when you hear high blood pressure, an accumulation of research is showing that too little calcium, potassium, and magnesium also plays an important role.'

(Jordan 1998: 728)

Likewise, in the concessive relation, the denial is implicit. For better understanding of the meanings of concessive relations, the reverse analysis may be done. Example (67) is based on the expectation that the capital city of a Canadian province, Quebec is one of the largest in the province. The concessive relation implies that there is such an expected conclusion, *the city is large,* which is being implicitly denied and then corrected by the information in the main clause, *it has a small population of just over half a million.* Although in example (67) both the conclusion and the denial are implicit, example (68) shows the implicit conclusion with explicit denial (Jordan 1998: 728).

(67) *Although* it is the provincial capital of Quebec, it has a small population of just over half a million

(Leisureways, 1995: 23; extracted from Jordan, 1998: 728)

(68) *Despite* a profusion of spandex and sequins, the black stage scene was *not* a pretty site

(Jordan 1998: 728)

In (68) above, the writer thought that readers would associate a profusion of spandex and sequins with a pretty site and denied this implicit expected conclusion explicitly (Jordan 1998: 728).

# IV Synchronic Distribution of English Concessives

# 4

# Synchronic Distribution of English Concessives

## 4.1 The Distribution of *though, although,* and *even though*

The distributional characteristics of the concessive *though* and *although* will be shown in this section. Our attention is given to the total frequency over written component and spoken component by using the BNC. The results are as follows:

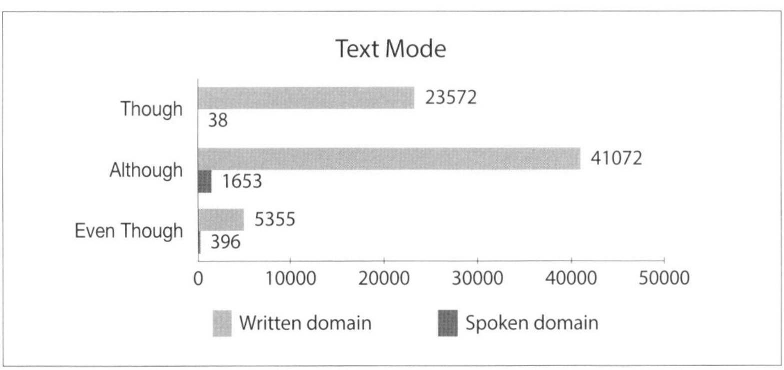

Figure 1. The Distribution of the Concessive Conjunctions *Though, Although*, and *Even Though* over the Text Modes of the BNC

As for the total[1] instances of three concessives, Figure 1 displays the difference of frequency over the text modes. While *even though* is employed just as 5,355 instances, the concessive *although* exhibits 41,072 cases in the written domain with the highest frequency.

A further important distinction can be noted with respect to spoken domain. The frequency in the spoken domain of concessives *though*, *although*, and *even though* is 38 cases (0.16%), 1,653 cases (3.87%), and 396 cases (6.89%) respectively. Thus the concept of concession is clearly less likely to be expressed in spoken language as shown in Figure 1.

Figure 2 gives an overview of the distribution of three concessives over the nine domains in the written component as well as spoken component.

---

1) As for the conjunction *though*, the total hits in the BNC are 34,370 which include the instances of *as though* and *even though*. Thus, to sift out the conjunction *though* out of 34,370 cases, the instances of *as though* (5,009) and *even though* (5,751) are eliminated, and then the total instances of the conjunction *though* are analyzed as 23,610.

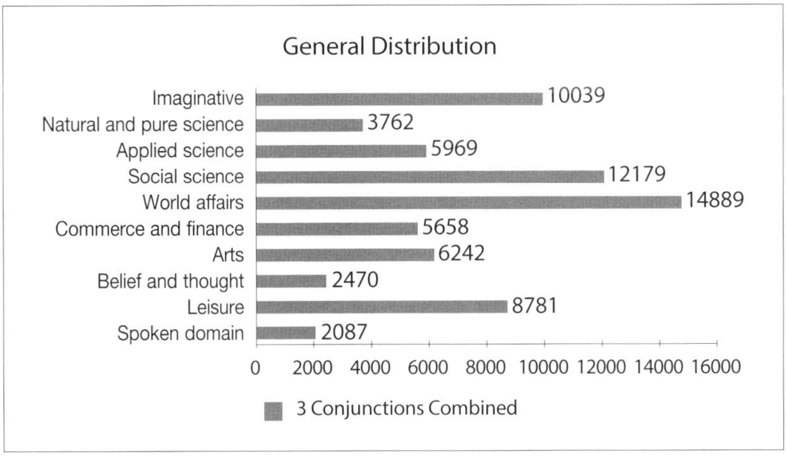


Figure 2. The General Distribution of the Three Concessive Conjunctions over the Text Domains of the BNC

As is instantly visible, considerable differences are found between the individual domains. 'World affairs' and 'Social science' domains exhibit the highest frequency in the use of the concessives *though*, *although*, and *even though*, while 'belief & thought' is the category with the lowest frequency in the written component of the corpus. A more detailed description of the distributional properties of three concessives are discussed in the following section. Figures 3, 4, and 5 display the distribution of the three above-mentioned concessive conjunctions over the same 9 text-domains. The order of the categories is the same in all three charts in order to allow easy comparison.

As shown in Figure 3, it is immediately noticeable that the conjunction *though* is most commonly employed in 'Imaginative' prose (5,218 cases) in the written domains. It occurs with the highest frequency, compared to the other categories. Consider the example in (69) in 'Imaginative' prose.

(69) She tried to think into motherhood, *though* Jeremy was twenty-five.

→ Imaginative domain (BNC: A0L 1515)

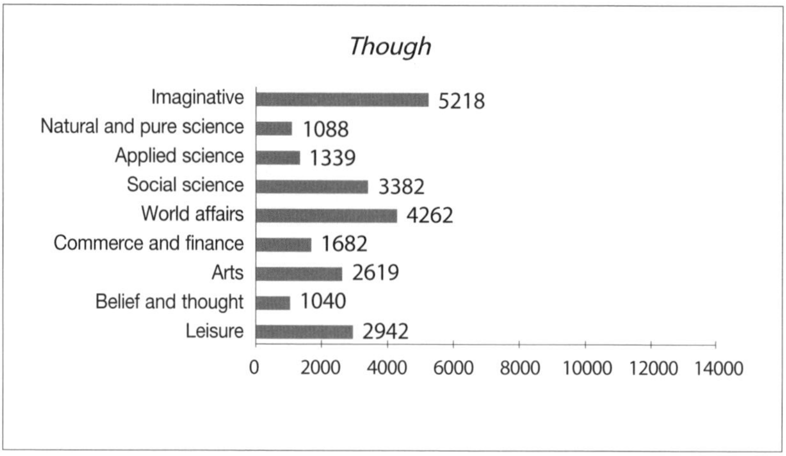


Figure 3. The Distributional Pattern of the Concessive Conjunction *Though* over the Domains of the BNC

Social science (3,382, cases) and 'World affairs' (4,262 cases) contain relatively plentiful instances compared to other informative texts. This kind of highly domain-specific use is typical of the three concessive conjunctions *though*, *although*, and *even though* as mentioned above. In addition, 'Belief and thought' contains the least instances (1,040 cases). The domain 'Leisure' has the third highest frequency in the informative texts of the different categories. This feature is also captured in Figure 4 below.

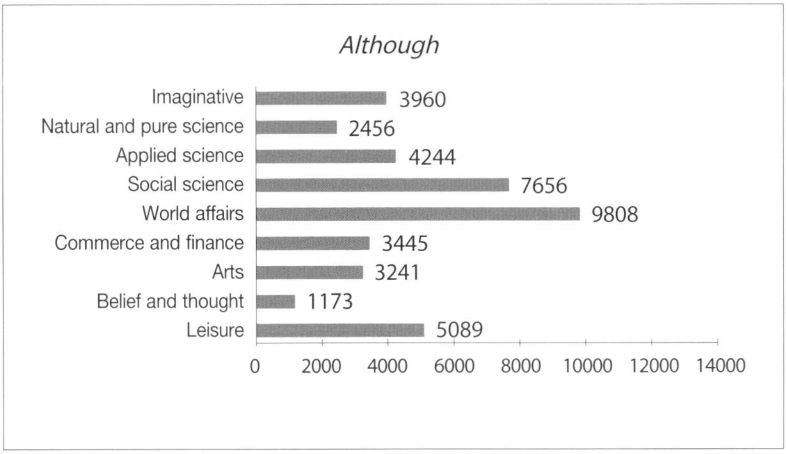


Figure 4. The Distributional Pattern of the Concessive Conjunction *Although* over the Domains of the BNC

Specifically, 'World affairs' exhibits the highest frequency with 9,808 instances. Again, the third highest frequency of *although* (5,089 occurrences) is in the domain of 'Leisure'. The lowest frequent usage is attested in the domain of 'Belief and thought' (1,173 cases). The example (70) involves 'World affairs' domain.

(70) *Although* the new chairman Sir Robert Reid had his critics, at the decade's end it was clear that his method of management had produced decisive changes. → World affairs domain (BNC: A11 177)

Let us look at the frequency of the conjunction *even though* below:

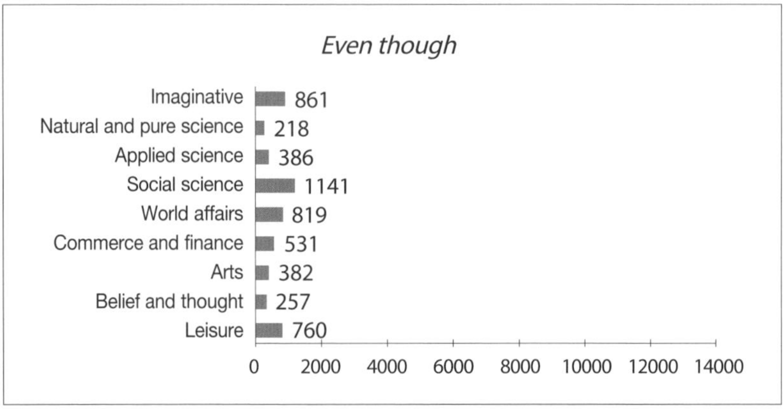


Figure 5. The Distributional Pattern of the Concessive Conjunction *Even though* over the Domains of the BNC

*Even though* occurs with the least frequency in the 'Natural and pure science' domain (218 cases) which is similar in its frequency in the instances of 'Belief and thought' (257 cases). The following example is excerpted from 'Social science' texts.

(71) 'Most churches are completely unprepared for the shock of finding an established member of the congregation is infected with HIV or dying with AIDS, *even though* this is increasingly common.'

→ Social science domain (BNC: A00 131)

On the whole, the conjunction *although* displays the most varied picture as shown in Figure 5. It exhibits a relatively balanced distribution over the various written text domains except the two domains of 'World affairs' and 'Social science' which are common denominators with the highest frequency of three conjunctions. The conjunctions *though* and *even though* show similar distributional patterns over written domains.

## 4.2 Functional Interpretation

There are textual preferences for *though*, *although*, and *even though* as shown in Figure 6. As Figure 6 represents, *though* is favored in the 'Imaginative' domain whereas *although* is preferred in informative texts including 'Natural and pure science', 'Applied science' and 'Social science' domains. These tendencies are due to functional 'specialization' (cf. Hopper 1991).

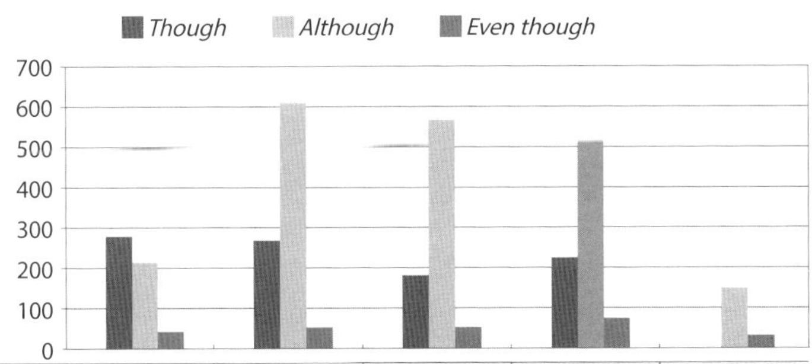


| Concessives | Imaginative | Natural and pure science | Applied science | Social science | Spoken domain |
|---|---|---|---|---|---|
| *Though* | 260 | 250 | 170 | 210 | 3 |
| *Although* | 200 | 570 | 530 | 480 | 140 |
| *Even though* | 40 | 50 | 50 | 70 | 30 |

Figure 6. The Frequency per Million Words over *Though*, *Although*, and *Even Though*

According to Chen (2000: 104), it is argued that "*although* had nearly reached its goal [as a factual concessive subordinator] by the end of the EModE period, but it would take *though* another several centuries to complete the process, for its hypothetical concessive use can be found as late as in 1900 (cf. Visser 1972, II: 905)." The conjunction *although* had been specialized as a factual concessive marker. That *although* is favored for factuality is due to an emphatic universal quantifier *all* which is an expression of totality or extremity. Information is more related with factuality, so *although* as a factual marker is used a lot in informative texts.

As shown in Figure 6, the frequency of *although* in informative texts such as 'Natural & Pure science', 'Applied Science', and 'Social Science' domains doubles in quantity, compared to the frequency of *though* in the same domains; conversely, its frequency in imaginative texts is the lowest in the written domains (200 occurrences). The reason for this phenomenon is that the informative texts such as in 'Natural and Pure science'. 'Applied Science', and 'Social Science' are more factual than imaginative texts.

Contrary to the conjunction *although,* concessive *though* is mainly employed in the imaginative texts (260). Imaginative prose comprises texts "which are fictional or which are generally perceived to be literary or creative" (Burnard 2000: 7). Thus, it can be said that it is less factual and informal than informative texts. Accordingly, *though* is preferred in the informal texts than *although* as the distributional characteristics show. We can confirm the statement of Quirk *et al.* (1986) that *although* and *though* are the most versatile of the subordinators.

Interestingly, Figure 6 shows that the usage preference of the conjunction *though* over the spoken domain is least in its distributional pattern (3 cases). The conjunction *though* is seldom used in the spoken domain compared to the conjunctions *although* (140 cases) and *even though* (30 cases). Analyzing the functions of the discourse marker *though* by using the spoken corpus MICASE, the hits of all types of *though*—without the distinctions of the parts of speech—were 335, only 7 (2.09%) of which were the conjunction *though*. It can be said that the conjunction *though* is less preferred in the spoken domain than the conjunctions *although* and *even though*. It can be postulated that the speakers use *although* and *even though* to emphasize their assertion in the spoken domain.

## 4.3 The Distribution of *while*

The total hits of *while* used as either the temporal or concessive conjunction are 47,105 occurrences in the written domains. Figure 7 represents total uses in written domains for either the temporal

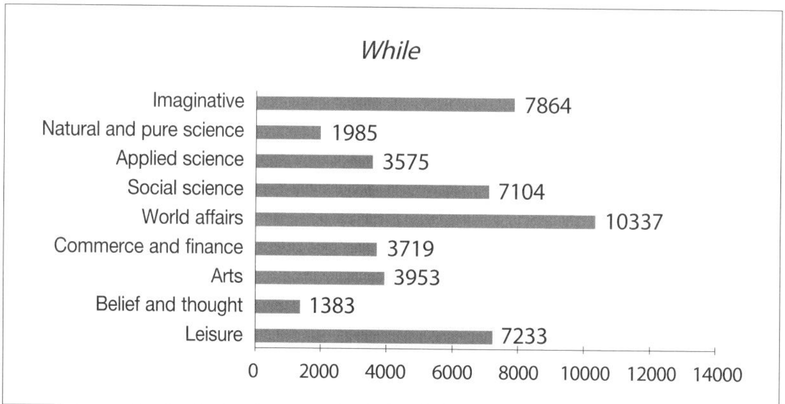


Figure 7. The Distributional Pattern of *While* as a Temporal or as a Concessive Conjunction over the Domains of the BNC

or concessive conjunction.

The use of frequency in 'World affairs' is the highest (10,337 occurrences), but 47,105 occurrences include all of temporal or concessive conjunctional uses. For the difficulty to analyze all the 47,105 cases in sorting out concessive use, certain occurrences[2)] are chosen and used for the analysis.

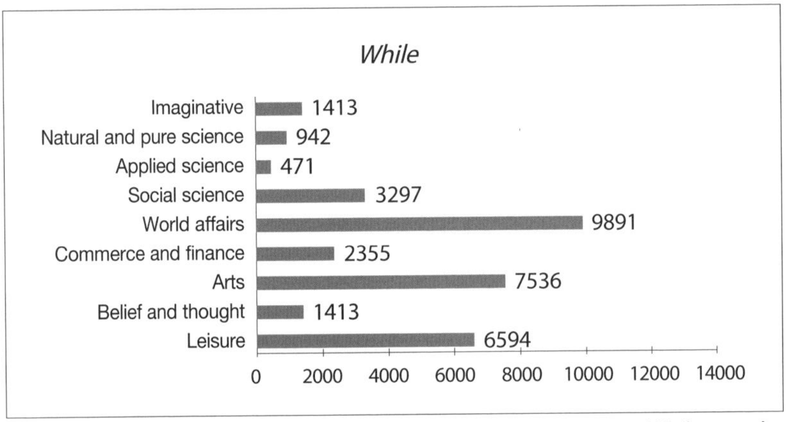


Figure 8. The Distributional Pattern of the Concessive Conjunction *While* over the Domains of the BNC

Worth noticing that concessive *while* is used with the highest frequency in the 'World affairs' domain as in Figure 8. The next two domains with high frequency are 'Arts' and 'Leisure.' The examples in (72)-(74) are extracted from the BNC.

2) Taken one per one source text, one hundred cases are chosen and analyzed. The figures shown in the chart of Figure 8 are multiplied by 471. However, out of 47,105 cases, only a small amount of the total hits are taken to sort out tokens of *while* as a concessive conjunction and that they are normalized by multiplication of 471 is a potential weak point of this analysis.

(72) Do art historians write about the past, *while* art critics write about the present? → Leisure

(BNC: A04 65)

(73) It's significant, too, that *while* Herbert Tree was laying the foundations of drama training in England, the famous partnership of Stanislavsky and Danchenko in Russia was beginning, and saw the first developments towards the establishment of the Moscow Arts Theatre. → Arts

(BNC: A06 142)

(74) Mikhail Shchadov, the Minister for Coal, told the Trud newspaper yesterday that so far this year, deliveries were 18.5 million tonnes less than planned, *while* 35 million tonnes of mined coal was lying at pitheads for want of freight rolling-stock. → World Affairs

(BNC: A1P 100)

The textual preference for "World affairs" is also interpreted as 'specialization' (cf. Hopper 1991) of *while* as the concessive conjunction.

## 4.4 The Distribution of *whereas*

The total hits of *whereas* are 6,163 occurrences. Figure 9 demonstrates the text mode of *whereas*. The total number of occurrences is relatively low compared to *though*, *although*, and *while*. This low frequency is due to 'persistence' and 'specialization' (cf. Hopper 1991). Like other concessive conjunctions, its uses in the spoken text are less frequent than in the written text. The usage pattern of *whereas* over the written domains is as follows in Figure 10.

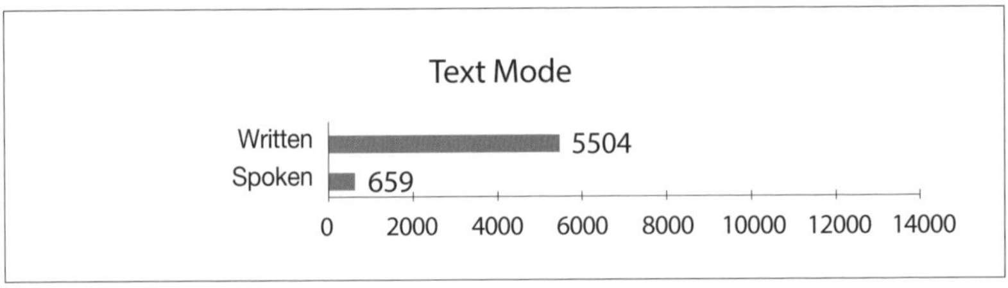


Figure 9. The Distribution of the Concessive Conjunction *Whereas* over the Text Mode of the BNC

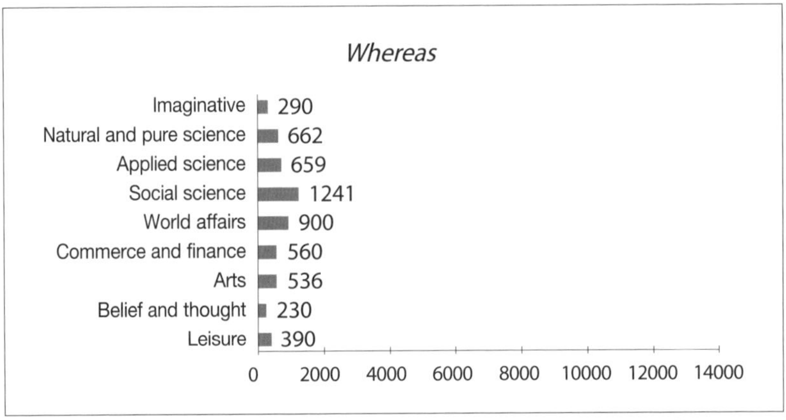


Figure 10. The Distributional Pattern of the Concessive Conjunction *Whereas* over the Domains of the BNC

It is visibly noticeable that *whereas* occurs with the highest frequency in the 'Social Science' domain. As indicated in the OED, when *whereas* means 'in view of the fact that' or 'inasmuch as', it is "chiefly, now only introducing a preamble or recital in a legal or other formal document." The example in (75) is taken from the 'Social Science' domain in the BNC.

(75) He estimates that an executive sous-chef working in a top London restaurant or hotel would be earning between £25,000 and £27,000, *whereas* a head chef in contract catering at a director's dining room, for example, would be doing very well to earn £20,000.

(BNC: A0C 1373)

The reason for this restrictive use in the 'Social Science' domain is associated with the source of *where*. One source word of *where* had meaning of 'it being the case that' and 'in view of the fact that' mainly in legal or other formal documents, but this function of *where* is obsolete according to the OED, and *whereas* takes over that function. This restriction in use can be interpreted as 'persistence' (cf. Hopper 1991). In addition, the use in the special genre 'Social Science' is attributed to its 'specialization' (cf. Hopper 1991) Because of preference in the legal contexts, its total frequency is relatively low.

## 4.5 The Distribution of *however*

The total number of hits of *however* as a conjunction is 5,049 occurrences. The frequency of *however* in the written domain is 4,788 whereas its frequency in the spoken domain is 261. Let us look at Figure 11 and Figure 12 below. Figure 11 displays the distribution of *however* over the text mode, and Figure 12 shows its frequency over the written domains.

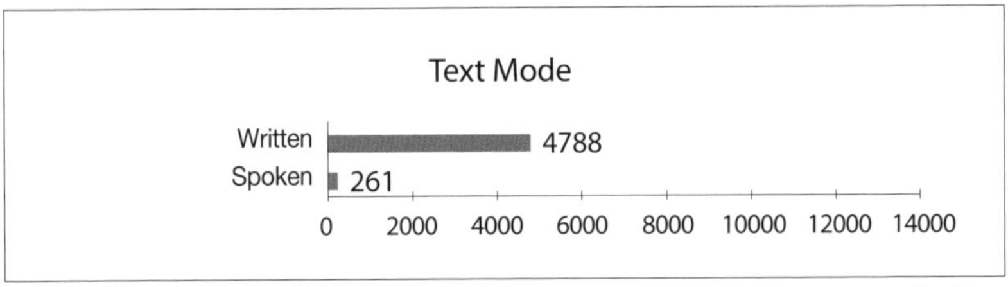


Figure 11. The Distribution of the Concessive Conjunction *however* over the Text Mode of the BNC

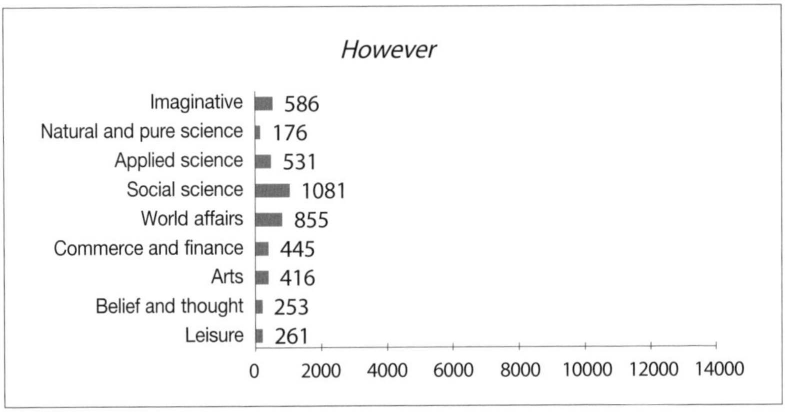


Figure 12. The Distributional Pattern of the Concessive Conjunction *However* over the Domains of the BNC

As Figure 11 represents, *however* in the text mode is surely favored in written domains. The highest frequency for *however* is in 'Social Science.' The example in (76) is extracted from 'Social Science' domain in the BNC.

(76) And, just as in May, Mr Gorbachev seems trapped. *However* much he might like to duck out, he cannot.

→ Social science (BNC: A2M 135)

Total frequency is the lowest among the concessive conjunctions derived from concomitance. As the OED states, its use as a conjunction is obsolete. Let us look at Figure 13 which is the distributional pattern of the adverb *however* over the written domains.

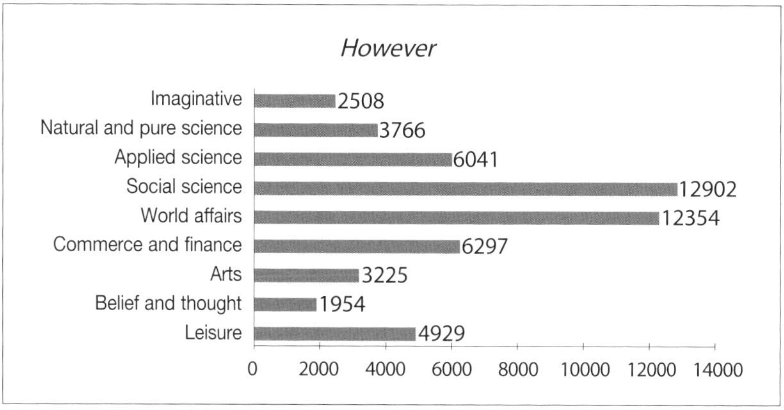


Figure 13. The Distributional Pattern of the adverb *However* over the Domains of the BNC

The total number of hits as an adverb is 54,636 cases, of which are 54,006 cases for the written domains. *However* as an adverb occurs with the highest frequency in 'Social Science' as well. The example in (77) below is taken out of the 'Social Science' domain.

(77) Between 1984 and 1986 those with AIDS died on average some ten months after diagnosis. Between 1987 and 1989, *however*, the survival period has already doubled to twenty moths.

→ Social science (BNC: A00 254)

The total number of hits as an adverb is almost ten times more than those as a conjunction. *However* as a conjunction was first attested in 1591 and as an adverb in 1623. Despite the similar period of emergence, its adverbial use is dominant. It is hypothesized that the obsolete use of *however* as a conjunction is because of its specialized use as an adverb. As an adverb, *however* modifies a sentence or clause as a whole; that is, *however* has functions similar to *nevertheless*, *notwithstanding*, etc.

# V Concessive as a Discourse Marker

# 5

# Concessive as a Discourse Marker

## 5.1 Discourse Marker

The definition and terminology of discourse markers (DMs) are still a debatable issue among scholars. Fraser (1990) mentions that although most scholars have agreed that DMs join discourse elements toghether, and they are still undecided on their definitions and functions. In other words, linguists are still unsure about giving DMs a universal term and a defined set of functions. Schiffrin (1987: 31) defines DMs as "sequentially dependent elements which bracket units of talk that signal relationships between immediately adjacent units of talk, and which have thus a coherence building function on a local coherence level." Fraser (1990: 387) define DMs as "a class of expressions, each of which signals how the speaker intends the basic message that follows to relate to the prior discourse." Lenk (1998: 246) defines DMs as "the term discourse marker refers only to expressions in spoken discourse that are used pragmatically, with a structuring and organizational function." Andersen (2001) defines DMs as a class of short linguistic elements that usually don't have much lexical meaning in them but carry a pragmatic meaning when used in oral discourse. Although most definitions offered by linguists seem to be close, there are still some slight differences among them (Rousan 2015: 35).

In addition, discourse markers have been assigned labels by different researchers such as 'discourse particles'(Aijmer 2002), 'discourse formatives'(Fraser 1987), 'discourse markers'(Fraser 1993), 'discourse operators'(Redeker 1991), 'discourse connectives' (Blackmore, 1987), 'pragmatic particles'(Ostman 1995), and 'pragmatic markers'(Andersen, 2001) among others. All the aforementioned terms signal a relationship between elements of a discourse (Rousan 2015: 35).

For many scholars such as Blakemore (1987), Redeker (1990) and Fraser (1988), the central function of discourse markers is to express the relation or relevance of an utterance to the preceding utterance or to the context. Others such as Keller (1979) see the central function of discourse markers as primarily structural. Levinson (1983) defines discourse markers as response signals. A discourse marker may also be a means to achieve conversational contiguity (Brown 1977). In addition, discourse markers are considered "essentially interactive" (Stubbs 1983: 70).

The features for discourse markers such as *now*, *anyway,* and *well* are also found with *though*. Among them is the function of indicating the relationship between an utterance and the surrounding discourse (Levinson 1983; Schiffrin 1987; Fraser 1988, 1990). In other words, discourse marker *though* indicates a contrast between two topics (Barth-Weingarten and Couper-Kuhlen 2002). It "instructs the recipient as to how to process the following stretch of discourse with respect to what has preceded" (Blakemore 1987; Brinton 1996). Other characteristics for a discourse marker are being a lexical adjunct, independent of the utterance in the sense that it can be removed without rendering the utterance non-understandable (Fraser 1988), resistant to truth-conditional treatment (Levinson 1983; Traugott 1999), and syntactically mobile (cf. Fraser 1988). Those characteristics can be also found with discourse marker *though*.

According to Brinton (1996: 29), the discourse functions fall broadly into two categories: textual and interpersonal. First, Brinton (1996: 38) further argues that in the "textual" mode, the speaker structures meaning as text, creating cohesive passages of discourse; it is "language as relevance," using language in a way that is relevant to context. The following falls to textual function: To indicate a new topic, a partial shift in topic (correction, elaboration, specification, expansion), or the resumption of an earlier topic (after interruption) according to Brinton (1996: 38).

Second, the "interpersonal" mode is the expression of the speaker's attitudes, evaluations, judgements, expectations, and demands, as well as of the nature of the social exchange, the role of the speaker and the role assigned to the hearer as discussed in Brinton (1996: 38). She further argues that in the interpersonal mode, discourse markers can be used subjectively to express responses or reactions to the preceding discourse or attitudes toward the following discourse. Further, they can be used interpersonally to effect cooperaton, sharing, or intimacy between speaker and hearer, including confirming shared assumptions, checking or expressing understanding, requesting confirmation, expressing difference, or saving face (Brinton 1996: 38-40).

## 5.2 Discourse-based Studies for *though*

Barth-Weingarten and Couper-Kuhlen (2002) propose that *though* functions as a marker of topic shifter, signalling the connection between two chunks of discourse and thereby linking them. The example (14) is taken from an American English radio talk show with Carla Perez on how to advise young men about whether to enlist for service in the Gulf War. Her guest, Sharon, describes the situation in her house, where one of her two sons wants to leave but the other does not. She herself is a pacifist. Let us take a look at (78).

(78) Carla Perez 23: Listen (Dat:50:15-50:48)[3]

C: death has no other TRACK.
S: that's RIGHT;
me- chIldren make mistA:kes,
and a part of RAIsing them,
is to-
acCEPT their mistAkes,
and help them corRECT their mistAkes,
and LEARN from their mistAkes.
but if thIs kid makes a mistAke on THIS one,
he may not have a CHANCE to corrEct it.
C: .hh uh LISten,
anOther factor ***though*** YOU brought up,=
uh because uh un (.) you sAID that what YOU know of the-
the pEOple who did NOT go in the vietnAm war,
that THEY suffered scars of NOT going in,
just b'cause their peers DID go in.

---

3) *Transcription conventions* used by Bath Weingarten and Couper-Kuhlen (2002)

| | | | |
|---|---|---|---|
| ACcent | primary accent | | |
| Accent | secondary accent | = | latching |
| . | final intonation falling to low | : | lengthening |
| ; | final intonation falling to mid | .hh | in-breath |
| ? | final intonation rising to high | (h) | laugh particle |
| , | final intonation rising to mid | (.) | pause |
| - | final level intonation | / | break-off |
| | | ( ) | suggested transcription |
| | | (( )) | meta-comment |
| | | [ | overlap |
| one line | one intonation unit | | (sub)topic 2 |

so that y- y- you're DAMNED if you do
DAMNED if you dOn't.
S: you're DAMNED if you do an' DAMNED if you don't in a LOT
of ways.

(Barth-Weingarten and Couper-Kuhlen 2002: 351)

Having talked for quite some time about the dilemma Sharon finds herself in, Carla Perez now shifts the topic in lines 11-12 to the situation the young men themselves experience (Barth-Weingarten and Couper-Kuhlen 2002). Barth-Weingarten and Couper-Kuhlen (2002) claim that this is done rather explicitly with an in-breath, the filler *uh*, the attention-getter *listen* and the phrase *another factor*, which is followed by *though*. Here we can also observe an incompatibility. However, it is no longer construable at the propositional level between two clause-sized units, X and Y[4], but it is rather a contrast on the textual level between two topics or subtopics (Barth-Weingarten and Couper-Kuhlen 2002).

The material of the new subtopic is indicated by shading grey.

---

4) Barth-Weingarten and Couper-Kuhlen (2002) schematically argue for the prototypical concessive relation as below:
*Cardinal Concessive pattern*:
*A*: *X* (claim)
*B*: *X′* (acknowledgement of claim)
*Y* (counterclaim)
*where X and Y are understood by participants to be potentially incompatible*
They call this pattern the Cardinal Concessive (cf. Couper-Kuhlen and Thompson 2000)

Barth-Weingarten and Couper-Kuhlen (2002) further state that in this example, *though* has lost its concessive function altogether and instead functions exclusively as a marker of topic organization, signalling the connection between and thereby linking two chunks of discourse. The textual function can be broadly paraphrased as 'let us now move on to *this* topic, while acknowledging what has been said on *that* topic' (Barth-Weingarten and Couper-Kuhlen 2002).

Ariel and Du Bois (2010) argue that the relations between concession and contrast in the context of the negotiation of stance alignment (Du Bois 2007) between participants in conversation. They discuss that an interlocutor using an initial *but* conjunction clearly frames her-or-his utterance as an act of divergent alignment with respect to a previous stance. They further claim that whereas both *but* and *though* mark opposition between concepts, this opposition may be interactionally foregrounded or downgraded. It appears that the initial *but* foregrounds the opposition, while the final *though* downgrades it (Ariel and Du Bois 2010). The example in (79) is extracted from Ariel and Du Bois (2010).

(79) KEN: I eat like,
.. you know,
.. vegetables,
and,
s- salads and,
JOANNE: [ (H)] That's the problem ***though***. (SBC015)

(Ariel and Du Bois (2010))

According to Ariel and Du Bois (2010), *but* increases the potential for a conflictual interpretation as a divergent stance, while *though* mitigates this like in (79), since the opposition is presented as a concession.

With the help of the studies of Barth-Weingarten and Couper-Kuhlen (2002) and Ariel and Du Bois (2010), how *though*, grammaticalized as a discourse marker, serves the function in discourse is examined in the following section.

## 5.3 Use of *though* across Positions

Discourse marker *though* is syntactically free and usually enclitic. The syntactic mobility leads us to assume that there may be differences across positions because *though* as a discourse marker can be technically located in the initial, the medial, or the final position. Therefore, this study was done on the assumption that *though* as a discourse marker serves different functions.

The present study made use of the MICASE corpus. The attribution can be controlled in this corpus for a specific purpose. This research limited the attribution to native speakers of American English with a highly interactive rating for discourse type.

There were 391 hits for *though* in this attribution. However, conjunctional use of introducing clauses such as *even though* and *as though,* the subordinate conjunction *though*, and *though* misspelled for *thought* in transcripts are included for the total numbers of matches; they were eventually excluded for the analysis. Therefore 335 tokens were selected and analyzed.

Of these 335 tokens are 56 tokens in medial position[5], and 279 tokens are in final position[6]. Unlike the assumption, there is no case in initial position, and final position is favored by *though*. Still, there is the assumption that *though* either in medial position or in final position may serve different functions. Next, the functions of *though* in respective position will be investigated in the following sections.

### 5.3.1 In Medial Position

*Though* in medial position functions to introduce the statement against the hearer's expectation which has been raised in the prior discourse. The example (80) illustrates this function. S1 is a male senior faculty member and S2 is a female senior undergraduate. S1 is advising about a Linguistics Independent Study.

(80)

1 **S2:** i found, one useful one from the web, most of 'em from the web were, um, there was something that was set up, as, a a conversational thing for, a linguistics class, and so it was just questions and replies [**S1:** oh i see. ] and there were four hundred and twenty-one entries

---

5) Medial position is the position like in '... *though* .....' Some tokens are classified to medial position because they are in the middle of the whole sentence, although they are in final position of the psuedo-cleft subject.

6) The tokens of final position can be either utterance- or clause-final, and they can be followed by some adverbs.

and the first_ <S1 LAUGH> out of the first fifty i think forty of them were **[S1:** oh okay ] were just, questions and replies that weren't too, helpful. **[S1:** uhuh ] but, i did find, i actually found something in Japanese that, if i could find some way to get it translated because the whole thing was on the conduit metaphor, and there were just random, um, translations, into English, every, third page or so, but.

**S1:** oh my word.

**S2:** yeah.

**S1:** wow. well, ask Jessica i guess.

**S2:** yeah. she said that she's not, **[S1:** that good? ] that good with characters. she's better with [speaking. so.

**S1:** [oh yeah.] could be. still there's lots of Japanese linguists.

**S2:** the most exciting thing i found ***though...*** is this. it's Wong Scollon and **[S1:** Scollon ] here's the, the first page of the abstract.

(MICASE ADV355SU094)

S2 found some interesting articles in Japanese, which she could not translate in English. Holding his floor, S1 in line 16 in (80) is saying "there's lots of Japanese linguists" because S1 thinks S2 pays attention to Japanese linguists since the topic on Japanese linguists continued in a previous discourse. However, against S1's expectation, S2 in lines 17 and 18 is more concerned in Cantonese American linguist Wong Scollon. *Though* is employed when the speaker brings up something into the discourse which is unexpected to the addressee (Lee 2010: 300).

In medial position, *though* also indicates that the speaker is involved in a specific speech act, especially of a face threatening act. *Though* in this position has a function of mitigating opposition of a speaker to the preceding statement. In (81), S1 is a junior faculty member, and S9 is a junior undergraduate in the class of Sex, Gender, and the Body Lecture.

(81)

S9: i personally like don't buy the whole, like soft porn [S1: mhm ] less porn thing like, [S1: okay ] um part of it like from my perspective is like s- it's like, when, it's like sexuality is being bought almost [S1: mhm ] like when that like you're just, if somebody's just as much exposing, i mean it's definitely like in a different manner from what i've like, from what i know of <S8: CELL PHONE RINGS> the controversy about Hustler, and stuff like that it that it th- like, they show a lot more, [S8: sorry ] i guess it's like the nude versus naked thing i don't really know but, [S1: okay ] i don't_ i still think that, it's pornography regardless.

S1: okay so pl- um so you wouldn't n- necessarily draw a line then, between Playboy

S9: well i mean i think ***though*** that there's definitely a difference between the types of pornography but i don't think it makes it any less, like ob- objectifying towards anybody (xx.)

(MICASE LES565SU137)

In line 13 in (81), in response to the utterance of S1, 'you wouldn't necessarily draw a line between the types of pornography,' S9 confronts S1, implying that there is definitely a difference. With the other discourse markers *well* and *I mean*, *though* also mitigates her opposition. Likewise *though* mitigates the potential for a conflictual interpretation (Ariel and Du Bois 2010; Lee 2010).

In addition to the function as a disagreeing marker, *though* has a function of a topic shifter in medial position. The conversation is taken from Statistics Office Hours in the MICASE corpus.

(82)

S1: let's see what the result is <PAUSE:05> oh they don't okay, um what do you get overall for your test statistic... in two-point-two-three?

S7: um i didn't i didn't do it cuz i didn't know.

S1: okay.

S6: negative-two-point-five-seven.

S1: mkay negative-two-point-five-seven, is good? [S3: how do yo- ] mhm, negative-two-point-five-seven, is your test statistic. [S7: mhm ] you wanna still find the P-values you normally would, and then, point-O-five is a good rule of thumb to use in general. what i would do ***though*** is check the answer with both one five and ten percent all three, because then you might say well if i make the decision that it's the same for all three of those then i pretty much know what my decision should be, okay?

S3: could i see the answer for four-point-nine?

(MICASE OFC575MU046)

Sl is an instructor, and S6 and S7 are students. S1, having talked about the test statistic result, shifts the topic to a subtopic to check the answer, the related one with the current topic in lines 9-10 in (82). When a topic or subtopic is changed, pseudo cleft constructions, such as *what surprises me though is* and *what I want you to do though*, are used by a speaker as in lines 9-10.

In sum, *though* as a discourse marker in medial position serves interpersonal and textual functions. and therefore it has a multifunctional profile.

### 5.3.2 In Final Position

Final *though* is also employed to introduce the statement against the hearer's expectation which has been raised in the previous discourse, similar to medial *though*. For instance, *though* in the example (83) indicates that the speaker's utterance does not match the hearer's expectation (Lee 2010).

(83)

1 **S1:** okay... alright... aw that, doesn't seem that [**S2:** doesn't seem too, huge.] it would be like too difficult, no. huh'uh. and they all getting the same variants on the same questionnaire, everything's in English, you're not gonna do the translation task, uh, there's only those two

tasks, you can, randomize it without any difficulty, uh yeah. and then yes i would say, that's a pretty simple protocol. um, have you, looked into, what, statistical tools you're planning to get out of this? i mean to to use with it?

**S2:** i haven't looked at that yet.

**S1:** okay. um

**S2:** i did some psych research and used, S-P-S-S to find statistical significance, so i'm familiar, with it. i would like to take, Stats four-oh-two ***though***, [maybe this summer?]

**S1:** [okay.] well when you get results, um, you can always go over to the stat lab, and uh ask to talk to a 25 consultant.

(MICASE ADV355SU094)

S1 is counseling on a Linguistics Independent Study. When S1 asks S2 what statistical tools she will utilize to deal with the data in line 8, she states that she did psychology research in line 11 and used S-P-S-S to figure out statistical significance in line 12. When the hearer S1 is told that S2 is familiar with S-P-S-S, S1 expects that S2 will use this tool. However, contrary to S1's expectation, S2 wants to take Stats four-oh-two in line 13. Thus, *though* in final position is employed to indicate the hearer's counter-expectation (Lee 2010: 310).

Next, *though* in final position can be used to signal disagreement. It is employed when the speaker contradicts, or disagrees with the hearer. In such face-threatening acts, *though* also functions as a pragmatic softener (i.e. as a face-saving strategy) (Lee 2010). Let us look at the example below.

(84)

**S2:** [i don't, i think the] problem is with the ques- the wording is like, what practical guidance to each of the axioms give us?

**S1:** knowing the axioms.

**S2:** i would say that the, g- axioms themselves don't give us any guidance,
[whatsoever.

**S1:** [i think they] do ***though*** i mean, like i i think [they do

**S2:** [an axiom] just is i mean it's like existence just is it doesn't, tell you anything, **[S4:** well ] you know.

**S1:** [no but knowing (xx)

(MICASE SGR999MX115)

The example (84) is a part of discourses among five students taken from Objectivism Student Group. Sl and S2 are senior graduate students In line 5, S2 is saying that "axioms themselves don't give us any guidance, whatsoever." Sl, however, says "they do" in line 7, and Sl disagrees with S2. Therefore, *though* as a pragmatic softener is employed to save face for S2 (Lee 2010: 302). In these cases of face threatening acts, *though* is accompanied by *well*, *I mean*, *I think*, or *like* as in (84) to mitigate a speaker's opposite opinion. Sometimes tag questions are added to invite an agreement of a hearer.

Beside, *though* is used to correct the speaker's own statement just said before. Let us look at the example (85). Students are talking about a woman. In line 6, S2 says that "she's always in that."

After that, S2 soon repairs his own statement from *always* to *usually* in line 9.

In addition to the function of softening face-threatening acts such as disagreeing with the previous speaker or the addressee, final *though* can serve the function of introducing a new topic, or of shifting the focus or perspective on the ongoing topic. The function of *though* here is to shift the focus on the current topic (Barth-Weingarten and Couper-Kuhlen 2002; Lee 2010). Let us consider the following example:

(85)

**S3**: can we do this one next?
**S1**: <LAUGH> can we do this one
**S4**: Lucky do you know if G-S-I office hours are always in alcove 5, or
**S1**: i don't know
**S3**: she's wherever, she goes wherever she can find one
**S2**: she's always in that
**S4**: oh really?
**S3**: well yeah
**S2**: usually she's in that one ***though***
**S3**: usually but, like s- she, it was there last week that's why i wish she could
**S1**: yeah i always s- i hear her over here sometimes
**S3**: that's why i wish she could find an empty spot. they kick someone out.

(MICASE SGR175SU123)

(86)

**S2**: well, the thing i- i don't know i thought they were the kind of the same number one, Buddhism and, you know Chinese philosophy, are a little different_ ah the philosophy was like a little obs- ob-scure to me. like uh the Chinese philosophy was just kind of

**S1**: what are you what are you, Taoism? Confucianism?

**S2**: yeah. all of it. like i just [**S1:** that's not so different from (Buddhism) ] i didn't have, i just didn't have, as much of an idea I don't think i liked it as well as Buddhism. and, then, also i j- i don't know what it was i the papers were different in length like the, Buddhism papers 10 were only two to three pages, whereas my Chinese philosophy were like eight, seven or eight, which might have something to do with it but, not a D minus worth.

**S3**: who were the other people in [your class? were they like upper-classmen? or were they

**S4**: [philosophy can be hard ***though*** it just seems so

(MICASE SEM300MU100)

S1 is a junior faculty member, and S2, S3 and S4 are undergraduates. They are talking about the grade S2 received. S2 got an A last semester, but she received D this time from the same professor. In lines 2 and 3 in (86), S2 is explaining her thought about Buddhism and Chinese philosophy and the strategy in which she coped with Buddhism and Chinese philosophy. After S2's utterance, S3 is asking whether there are upperclassmen in lines 13 and 14, and then, S4 returns to the previous topic, i.e. philosophy by using *though* in line 15. In this context, *though* functions as a topic shifter (Barth-Weingarten and Couper-Kuhlen 2002, Lee 2010: 303).

To sum up the functions of *though*, Table 15 shows the functions across position. *Though* in both medial and final position functions to set up statements against the hearer's expectation. Medial final *though*s have the functions of mitigating the opposition and repairing the speaker's previous utterance. In addition to the function of softening face-threatening acts, medial and final *though*s can serve the function of shifting the focus or perspective on the ongoing topic. In this regard, "*though* has the two-fold function in the textual and interpersonal domains" (Lee 2010: 305).

Table 15. The Functions of *Though* across Positions

| Functions | Position | |
|---|---|---|
| | Medial | Final |
| Introducing an Unexpected Statement | 12(21.4%) | 45 (16.1%) |
| Pragmatic Softener | 17(30.4%) | 104 (37.3%) |
| Topic Shifter | 24(42.9%) | 112 (40.1%) |
| Unclear or Unable to Analyse | 3 (5.4%) | 18 (6.5%) |
| Subtotal | 56(100%) | 279 (100%) |
| Total | 335 | |

Unlike the assumption that *though* as a discourse marker would have different functions across positions, there is no difference across positions as represented in Table 15. In addition, *though* is technically able to be in any position, but as a result of analysis, initial position is not favored by speakers. The reason that *though* as a discourse marker is not favored in initial position may be that a speaker is hesitant about using it in the beginning to save face for the hearer, because of the concessive meaning of *though*—to assert a speaker's opinion. Ariel and Du Bois (2010) similarly propose that interlocutors wish to downgrade the potential conflict, while still making their opposing point, and they may then opt for non-initial *though*.

### 5.3.3 Evaluation of Positional Claims

It is often said that discourse markers are "restricted to sentence-initial position, or may always occur sentence initially (Brinton 1996: 33). For Keller (1979: 222), this is one of the three defining characteristics of discourse markers. Unlike the claims of scholars (cf. Levinson 1983, Stubbs 1983, Schiffrin 1987, and Fraser 1988) advocating restriction to initial position as a necessary condition, the position of a discourse marker *though* is not found in initial position.

Other scholars (cf. Crystal and Davy 1975, Goldberg 1980, James 1983, and Aijmer 1986) point out discourse markers frequently appear sentence medially and finally as well. Following the results of these studies, we assumed that discourse markers in each position serve different functions. However, through the analysis, it is revealed that *though* as a discourse marker has no functional differences across positions.

In sum, this study based on individual positions reveals that a discourse marker is not supposed to be in initial position (cf. the term 'final *though*' in Barth-Weingarten and Couper-Kuhlen (2002) and the term 'non-initial *though*' in Ariel and Du Bois (2010)). Besides, this study confirms that discourse markers do not serve necessarily different functions even if their positions vary.

# VI Diachronic Developments of Concessives

# 6

# Diachronic Developments of Concessives

## 6.1 Literature Review

Given their great number and importance, previous studies on concession and resulting contributions to the issue of concession should not go unmentioned. The notion of concession seems to have already been well-known in earlier descriptions of grammar. Hermodsson (1994: 69) quotes from Samuel Shaw's *Grammatica Anglo-Romana* (1687) "Concessives… grant something which the following sentence may seem to oppose…." By surveying the literature by earlier scholars, the common semantic sources giving rise to grammaticalization of concessive markers will be identified. We will explain how the common semantic sources are related with concessive conjunctions under consideration.

Concessive markers may derive from a wide variety of sources (cf. König 1985, 1986, 1994, Heine *et al.* 1993, Traugott and König 1991, Chen 2000), all related in one way or another to the basic semantic, pragmatic, and syntactic properties of concessives. Many studies on concession have been researched cross-linguistically.

König (1985: 10) identifies various historical sources for concessive connectives by investigating the affinity between concessivity and other semantic domains; concessive connectives can be divided into four groups as below.

(87)

a.

Universal quantification: E. *although*, *ableit*, *for all, all the same*, *however, anyway*; G. *bei all, allerdings, wiewhol, zwar*; Lat. *quamquam (cf. quisquis* 'whoever'); F. *toutefois, tout...que, (com)bien que*; Finn. *vaikka* 'although' (cf. *vaikka kuka* 'whoever', *kuka 'who'* ); Dutch *ook al, hoewel*; Hung. *habar* 'although' (cf. *ha 'if', ki 'who', barki* 'whoever'); Russ. *vsë-taki, chotja*; Chin. *swei ran...dou/ye* 'although...all/also', etc.

b. Focus particle/emphatic particle and/or conditional/temporal conjunction: E. *even though*, *even so*; G. *ob-gleich, ob-whol, ob-schon, wenn-gleich, wenn...auch, obzwar*; Lat. *et-si*; Gk. *ei-kai*; Dutch *ofschoon*; F. *quand même*; Finn. *jos-kin* 'if-also', *sitten-kin* 'then-also'; Serb. Croat. *i-ako* 'also-if'; Jap. *keredo(mo)* 'though', *mo* 'also'; Malayalam *-enkil-um* 'if-so'; Ewe *néha* 'if-and'; Sesotho *le ha* 'and/even if', etc.

c. Remarkable co-occurrence/co-existence: E. *nevertheless*, *nonetheless, notwithstanding, just the same, regardless, still, yet*; G. *gleichwohl, dennoch, ungeachtet, unbeschadet*; Lat. *nihilo minus*; F. *tout de même*, *cependant, n'empêche que*; Sp. *aunque, con todo, todavia*; Turk. *bu-nunla beraber* 'together with this'; Hung. *mégis* 'still-too'; Jap. *nagara* 'while, although'; Dutch *niettemin, niettegenstaande*; Turk. *iken* 'while, though', etc.

d. 'Obstinacy, conflict, disorder': E. *in spite of, despite*; F. *en dépit de, au mé-pris de, mal-gré* (cf. *bon gré mal gré* 'willy-nilly'); G. *trotz, trotzdem*; Sp. *a pesar de* (*pesar* 'sorrow, regret'); Dutch. *ondanks* (*ondak* 'ingratitude'; Mid. Dutch *te enes ondanke* 'against somebody's will'), *in weerwil van* (cf. G. Widerwille); Arabic *raḡman* (*raḡama* 'compel'); Turk. *rağmen*, etc.

(König 1985: 10-11)

Traugott and König (1991: 199) argues that "among the major sources in the development of concessive markers are expressions whose original or at least earlier, meaning was 'concomitance' or 'co-occurrence', and certain negative expressions (cf. König 1985, 1986 & 1988)."

(88)

a. connectives originally expressing simultaneity or temporal/overlap: *while, still, yet*; Gm. *zugleich, indes (sen), dennoch*; Fr. *cependant*; Turk. *iken* 'while', 'although'; Indonesian *sekali-pun* 'although' (at the same time + even'); Hawaiian *oiai* 'while', 'meanhile', 'although'; Jap. *nagara* 'while', 'although'

b. connectives originally expressing simple cooccurrence or concomi-tance, or even similarity: EME *withal* (< 'along with the rest'), *all/just the same*; Gm. *gleichwohl, bei all*; Dan. *evenwel*; Rum. *cu toate ca* 'with all (things) that'); Turk. *bununla beraber* 'together with this'); Hopi *naama-*

*hin* 'although' (< 'together' + 'thus'); Quileute *-t'e* 'with, although'

c. negation of asymmetry (e.g. negation of opposition, negation of negative correlation): *notwithstanding, nevertheless, nonetheless*; Fr. *n'empeche que*; Gm. *nichtsdestoweniger*

(Taugott and König, 1991: 199)

In addition, Heine *et al.* (1993), by studying African languages, establish source-target lexicon, and list the source for concessive markers as below.

(89) Source-target lexicon

Cooccurrence ("concomitance") marker > concessive marker English *while, still, yet, at the same time* (Traugott & König, 1991). French *cependent* (Traugott & König, 1991)

(Heine *et al.* 1993: 60)

Besides, Chen (2000) classifies the sources into the following five categories that contributed to the development of concessive markers in Early Modern English, although the study is not conducted cross-linguistically:

(90)

a. Expressions that directly concede the existence of an adverse situation, such as *admit* and *grant*.

b. Expressions that emphasize the adversity of the conceded situation, such as *all* and *never so*.

c. Expressions that assert the ineffectiveness of the conceded situation, such as *in (de)spite of* and *notwithstanding*.

d. Expressions that state the concomitance of the two situations expressed by the antecedent and the consequent, such as *though*.

e. Expressions that help affirm the factuality of the situation expressed by the consequent, such as *nevertheless*, *still*, and *yet*.

(Chen, 2000: 91)

As for (90a), Chen (2000) claims that a concessive clause expresses the speech act of conceding, and conceding can be expressed directly by an expression containing a verb form. Through (87)-(90), we confirm that listed sources are grammaticalized to the different types of the concessive markers: conjunctive adverbs, prepositional phrases, and conjunctions. Adopting the findings in König (1985, 1986, 1994), Heine *et al.* (1993), Traugott and König (1991), and Chen (2000), we reclassify and diagram the sources of concessive markers in English in Figure 14. Unlike König (1985) and Traugott and König (1991), and Chen (2000), we group the source of few elements together as the source of concomitance and subdivide the source of concomitance into the circumstance, time, space, and manner, as shown in Figure 14.

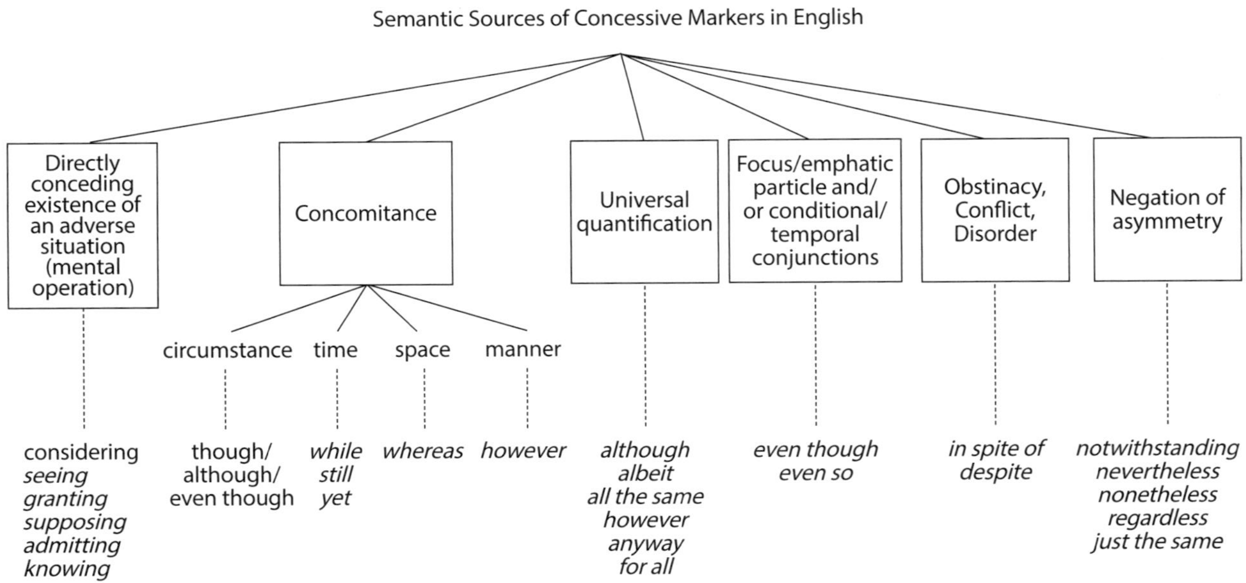


Figure 14. Semantic Sources of Concessive Markers in English

## 6.2 Grammaticalization Principles

Hopper (1991) proposes the following five principles largely subscribed to by students of grammaticalization: decategorialization, divergence, persistence, layering, and specialization. Decategorialization refers to the fact that forms that undergo grammaticalization tend to lose the characteristics of full categories (noun and verb) and assume attributes of secondary categories (adjective, participle, preposition, etc.). Divergence refers to the phenomenon that there are multiple forms sharing etymology but diverging functionally. Persistence refers to the phenomenon that a grammaticalized item retains the meaning of the source for a long time. Layering refers to the coexistence of the old layers with the new layers. Specialization refers to the narrowing of choices. Because five principles are related to the changes of markers in question, they will be mentioned in the following sections.

### 6.2.1 Decategorialization

Decategorialization is one of grammaticalization principles which Hopper proposed in 1991. In his paper, he defines it as below:

> Forms undergoing grammaticization[7] tend to lose or neutralize the morphological markers and syntactic privileges characteristic of the full cat-

7) The terminology of the subject is diverse. Some authors prefer "grammaticization" or even "grammatization" to "grammaticalization." However, the majority use "grammaticalization."

egories Noun and Verb, and to assume attributes characteristic of secondary categories such as Adjective, Participle, Preposition, etc.

(Hopper 1991: 22)

We will excerpt an example that shows a more general process of conceptual transfer from concrete nouns to closed-class. We can see this phenomenon with an example from the color domain (Heine 1997: 30). This development leads from nouns to adjective-like words. One of the most common conceptual sources for new color terms is provided by the plant domain, most of all by plant parts such as flowers and fruit. As we know in general, some examples of color terms (e.g., 'orange', 'violet') show that a lexeme denoting a plant part develops into the one denoting a color term since the noun gradually loses nominal properties and acquires features which can express qualities and modify other nouns.

The process concerned has been described by Heine *et al.* (1991) with reference to a categorial metaphor whereby a concept belonging to the domain of concrete items—the OBJECT domain in their terminology—serves as a structural template to express concepts belonging to the QUALITY domain. The implications of this conceptual transfer are that the relevant terms for plant parts lose nominal properties and increasingly acquire properties linking them with the category of adjectives. This example shows decategorialization from full categories to secondary categories.

### 6.2.2 Divergence

Hopper (1991) proposes 'the Principle of Divergence,' which is called Split by Heine and Reh (1984: 57-59). According to his definition (Hopper 1991: 24), "when a lexical form undergoes grammaticization to a clitic or affix, the original lexical form may remain as an autonomous element and undergo the same changes as ordinary lexical items." As a result of this principle, pairs or multiples of forms emerge from a common etymology. For instance, let us see the English indefinite article *a(n)* and the word *one*.

The latter was derived from the former, and consequently both have the same etymology. The resulted forms of them are phonologically different, and they make us opaque to comprehend the relationship between them compared to a case of phonologically identical forms.

Divergence is applicable to cases where one and the same autonomous lexical item becomes grammaticalized in one context and does not become grammaticalized in another. Examples of divergence from Malay are (91)-(93). In Malay, a classifier must precede nouns in certain discourse contexts.

(91) Ada-lah kami lihat tiga orang budak-budak kena hukum.

happen we see three<CL> boy-PL get punishment

'We happened to see three <CL> boys being punished.'

(Hopper 1986: 64)

(92) Maka pada suatu pagi kelihatan-lah sa-*buah* kapal rendah.

and on one morning was:seen-*lah* a-<CL> ship low

'Then one morning a <CL> low ship was sighted.'

(Hopper 1986: 77)

(93) Mati-lah tiga *ekor* tikus.

dead-*lah* three <CL> rat

'Three <CL> rats were killed.'

(Hopper 1986: 144)

According to Hopper (1986) and Hopper and Traugott (2003[1993]), in Malay, *orang, buah,* and *ekor* are classifiers. We can use the classifier *orang* before nouns that depict humans, *buah* before objects of a bulky size, and *ekor* before nouns denoting animals of any kind. Therefore, we cannot choose them interchangeably. In Malay, "most of the classifiers double as autonomous nouns" (Hopper and Traugott 2003[1993]: 120), schematically as in (94). *Orang, buah,* and *ekor* mean 'person, man,' 'fruit,' and 'tail' respectively. Thus, there is a divergence between a lexical meaning and a grammaticalized meaning.

(94) buah ('fruit') → buah ('fruit')
→ buah (classifier)

### 6.2.3 Persistence

'The Principle of Persistence' relates the meaning and function of a grammatical form to its history as a lexical morpheme according to Hopper (1991: 28). He further states that when a form undergoes grammaticalization from a lexical to a grammatical item, some traces of its original lexical meanings tend to adhere to its history, and details of its lexical history may be reflected in constraints on its grammatical distribution. He illustrates persistence by using the development in West African languages of object markers ("accusative cases") out of former serialized verbs such as *take*, provided by Lord (1982)'s discussion. In Gã (a Benue-Kwa language of West Africa), the form *k* is an accusative case marker in sentences such as:

(95) È k wòlò ŋmè-s

she OBJ book lay-down

'She laid the book down.'

(Lord, 1982: 118)

It was originally a verb meaning "take," which is moving toward grammaticalization as a case marker. Sentences such as these are historically of the type 'He took the book [and] laid [it] down,' and reflect a previous stage of polysemy of *k*, which could function either as a full verb "take" or as an accusative case marker. Certain restrictions on the distribution of this case marker can only be understood from the point of view of its origin in the meaning "take." Consider examples in the following:

(96) a. È ŋmè wl

she lay egg

'She laid an egg.'

b. *È k wl ŋmè

*she ACC egg lay

(Lord, 1982: 120)

The semantic relationship between the verb and object in 'laid down the book' is quite different from that in 'laid an egg.' In the first, the object is changed (moved, grasped, etc.) through the action of the verb; the object is 'affected' (Lord 1982, Hopper 1986).

In the second, the object is produced or brought about by the action of the verb; the object is 'effected.' The accusative case marker in Gã can only be used if the object is 'affected.' For this same reason, the accusative case marker *k* is inappropriate if the verb is one of experiencing. These kinds of constraints exist because Gã retains the restriction on the marking of direct objects which derives from the historical antecedent of this morpheme in the lexical verb 'to take': Only objects which can be 'taken' are marked morphologically as grammatical objects of the verb. This is exemplified for persistence (cf. Hopper 1991). That is, the grammaticalized construction is constrained by its origins (Hopper 1991, Hopper and Traugott 2003[1993]).

### 6.2.4 Layering

Hopper (1991: 22) claims that layering is that within a broad functional domain, new layers are continually emerging. As this happens, the older layers are not necessarily discarded, but may remain to coexist with and interact with the newer layers. This can be illustrated as in (97).

(97) $$A > \left\{ \begin{matrix} B \\ \\ A \end{matrix} \right\} > B$$

As shown above, an old layer and a new layer coexist. As a matter of fact, it is difficult to say A becomes B without the intermediary stage where A and B coexist.

This diversity comes about because when a new layer appears in a functional domain, it does not immediately (and may never) replace an already existing set of functionally equivalent forms. The tendency is that old and new layers coexist. Layering is the synchronic result of successive grammaticalization of forms which contribute to the same domain (Hopper and Traugott 2003[1993]: 125).

According to Lühr (1984), the tenses and aspects of English provide some good examples. In the past tense, it is possible to distinguish an archaic layer of vowel alternations in strong verbs like *drive/drove, take/took*. These formations coexist with a more recent layer making the use of an apical suffix [t] or [d], as in *notice/noticed, walk/walked*; this suffix was itself almost certainly derived from an auxiliary verb with the English *do*. In addition to the tense formations with phonological alternation and suffixation, a periphrastic construction involving *do/did* appears in questions, negatives, and emphatics. Related examples are shown in (98).

(98) a. *keep (on) + -ing*: He *keeps* (*on*) *signaling* to me. (iterative)

b. *go on + -ing*: He *went on asking* silly questions. (iterative)

c. *be about + to*: We *were about to* get on the plane. (prospective)

d. *start + to*: They *started to* laugh. (inceptive)

e. *take + to:* She *took to* criticizing his work habits. (inceptive)

(Hopper 1991: 23)

We often find that one of the competing forms predominates (i.e. specialization), and eventually extends its range of meanings to include those of the constructions which it replaces. The explanation of specialization dealt with in the following:

### 6.2.4 Specialization

Specialization refers to "the narrowing of choices that characterizes an emergent grammatical construction" (Hopper 1991: 25). Hopper (1991: 22) claims that as grammaticalization takes place, the variety of forms narrows and the smaller number of forms selected assume more general grammatical meanings.

In French, historically the original negator was *ne*, and nouns like *pas* 'step, pace' could strengthen the negation. The example (99) exemplifies the use of French negator *ne - pas*.

(99) Il ne boit pas de vin.
he NEG drinks NEG PARTIT wine
'He doesn't drink wine.'

(Hopper 1991: 26)

It can be assumed that the strengthening noun was once tailored to the nature of the verb; thus verbs of motion could be reinforced with *pas* as in *He doesn't go a step*, verbs of giving and eating with *mie* 'crumb' as in *He didn't eat a crumb*; and so on.

Gamillscheg (1957) lists a variety of adverbially used nouns denoting a least quantity of something used in Old French as the following:

(100) *pas* 'step, pace'
*point* 'dot, point'
*mie* 'crumb'
*gote* 'drop'
*amende* 'almond'
*areste* 'fish-bone'
*beloce* 'sloe'
*eschalope* 'pea-pod'

(Gamillscheg, 1957: 753)

Among adverbially used nouns in Old French, *pas, point, mie* and *goutte* predominated in the 16th century, and only *pas* and *point* were still in use by the modern period. From all of them, however, only *pas* is a true negator, in which it has overwhelmingly higher discourse frequency, and is the unmarked negator in the sense of being semantically neutral. For this reason, only *pas* has become a general negator. In the spoken language, the *ne* of ordinary verbal negation is usually dropped out (*je sais pas* 'I don' t know'), leaving *pas* as the only mark of negation. Thus, *pas* becomes specialized.

## 6.3 Grammaticalizaiton Mechanisms

Alongside the principles in the preceding sections, the involved mechanisms will be examined in order in the following sections as well. They are subjectification, analogy, metonymy, metaphor, and generalization.

### 6.3.1 Subjectivity vs Subjectification

The notion of subjectivity is related to Cognitive Grammar (see Langacker 1985, 1990, 1999, 2000). As the perspective of a speaker of an event or a situation is incorporated into its description, a subjective construal of the event or the situation arises. For instance, while (101a) implies objective construal of an event in that the child moves, (101b) represents subjective construal of an event because the speaker's point of view, not the mailbox is thought of moving. The conceptualization of motion arises in the directionality of the speaker's mental scanning along the path (Radden 1996: 450; Verhagen 2005).

(101) a. The child is hurrying across the street.

b. There is a mailbox across the street.

(Verhagen 2005: 1)

The cognitive approach to language description, however, is never uniform and the term 'subjectivity' has been employed in diverse ways. Traugott (1989, 1995, 199a, 199b) proposes that subjectivity is associated with the way in which the psychological or emotional perspective of a speaker about a situation or an event is incorporated into its description, as in the performative uses of locutionary verbs such as *I promise* and in the use of discourse markers such as *after all*. Her view on subjectivity is similar to Lyon's (1982: 102) in that subjectivity is related to "the locutionary agent's expression of himself and his own attitudes and beliefs." Nuyts (2001a, 2001b) also suggests that subjectivity is a characteristic of mental-state predicates such as *think* (Verhagen 2005).

Intersubjectivity is a notion associated not only with the speaker' s perspective but also with the way in which the speaker tries to take up the perspective of the hearer or to negotiate his or her own perspective with that of the hearer. Traugott (1999b) suggests "intersubjectivity crucially involves [the speaker's] attention to [the addressee] as a participant in the speech eent, not in the world talked about." Nuyts (2001a, 2001b) proposes that intersubjectivity describes evidential markers such as the epistemic adjective *probably,* indicating that some evidence which has a bearing on the situation is accessible to both the speaker and the hearer (Verhagen 2005).

However, Verhagen claims that intersubjectivity is concerned with a central characteristic of human communication, and language is not only a means for exchanging information about the state of the world, but also is associated with "connecting, differentiating, and tailoring the contents of points of view with respect to each other (rather than organizing a connection to the world)" (Verhagen 1986: 4). The central role of language is "to establish or modify the way in which individually relate to each other, and only derivatively to express how individuals perceive and understand the world." Intersubjectivity is the way of coordinating the points of view of a speaker and an addressee (Verhagen 1986: 2005).

In the sense of subjectification or 'speaker involvement' in Traugott (1982, 1986, 1988) and Traugott & König (1991), the extension of meanings is referential meaning toward subjective, 'speaker-based' attitudes and points of view. There are three kinds of semantic-pragmatic tendencies for semantic change in general as follows:

(1) Semantic-pragmatic Tendency I

Meanings based in the external described situation > meanings based in the internal (evaluative/perceptual/cognitive) situation

(2) Semantic-pragmatic Tendency II

Meanings based in the described external or internal situation > meanings based in the textual situation

(3 Semantic-pragmatic Tendency III

Meanings tend to become increasingly situated in the speaker's subjective belief-state/attitude toward the situation

(Traugott and König 1991: 208-209)

An instance of Tendency I is the extension of the originally spatial preposition *after* to the temporal preposition *after* in Old English: A shift from a reference to a concrete physical situation to a reference to a cognitive perceptual situation. An exemplar of Old English (OE) prepositional *after* 'following behind, later' to the Middle English (ME) subordinating *after* belongs to Tendency II. Then, in case of Tendency III, casuals, concessives, and particles of denial are all essential expressions of a speaker's view to propositions, for example of temporal *while* to concessive *while*.

### 6.3.2 Analogy

Analogy has been widely recognized as significant for change in general, most especially morpho-syntactic change. Analogy modifies surface manifestations and in itself does not affect rule change although it does influence rule spread either within the linguistic system itself or within the community (Hopper and Traugott 2003[1993]: 39). As discussed in Hopper and Traugott (2003[1993]), analogy means the attraction of extant forms to already existing constructions, and it is overt. Along different axes reanalysis and analogy can be distinguished. Unlike reanalysis operating along the "syntagmatic" axis of linear constituent structure, analogy operates along the "paradigmatic" axis of options at any one constituent node (Jakobson and Halle 1956, quoted by Hopper and

Traugott 2003[1993]).

Meillet (1958[1912]) asserts analogy can only operate when a nucleus of forms has already emerged to which new forms can be assimilated. In his rather narrow, local interpretation of analogy, which was defined as a process whereby irregularities in grammar, particularly at the morphological level, were regularized, this mechanism was seen as one of 'proportion' or 'equation'. However, the difficulty with the formula of proportion is that it gives no account of why one member of the pair is selected as the model. Kiparsky (1968), decades later, redefines analogy in phonology as rule extension, thereby giving a formal account of the fact that analogy is not random in language change. He views analogy as generalization or optimization of a rule from a relatively limited domain to a far broader one.

Even though it is said that only reanalysis can create new grammatical structures, the role of analogy should not be underestimated in the study of grammaticalization. The products of analogy are in many cases the prime evidence for speakers of a language that a change has taken place.

### 6.3.3 Metonymy vs Metaphor

Along with metaphor, metonymy is considered a major trigger of semantic changes. The reason of the rise of metonymy is due to a discourse pragmatic manipulation whereby concepts are subjected to contextual factors in utterance interpretation (Sperber and Wilson, 1986: 1). Heine *et al.* (1991) refer this process as 'context-induced reinterpretation.'

Anttila (1972: 142) claims that metaphor concerns semantic transfer through a similarity of sense perceptions, and is therefore analogical and iconic, while metonymy is semantic transfer through contiguity and is therefore indexical. Anttila proposes that metonymy points to semantic relations in certain contexts: contiguity in socio-physical or socio-cultural experience, contiguity in the utterance (that is, collocation), often ending in ellipsis, synecdoche (the part-whole relation).

Traugott and König (1991) extend the notion of metonymy from traditional concrete and overt contexts to cognitive and covert contexts, specifically the pragmatic contexts of conversational and conventional inference. The contiguity involved is based in the discourse world. The origin of the idea put forward by Traugott and König (1991) is to be found in Stern (1968[1931]). Stern views permutation (his term for metonymy) as resulting from "a word [being] used in a phrase where a notion in some way connected with its meaning is liable to form an element of the context" (Stern 1968: 353). He suggested that permutations result from "striving to fulfill as adequately as possible the symbolic and communicative functions of speech" (Stern 1968: 359); that is, a speaker's communicative intent and desire to be fully expressive is central.

In Heine *et al.* (1991), they view metonymy as gradual and continuous rather than discrete and discontinuous, compared to metaphor, which is a conceptual process which involves a transfer in discrete steps from one cognitive domain to another.

Traugott and König (1991: 194) claim that metaphor and metonymy correlate with shifts to different types of grammatical function: "Metaphor is largely correlated with shifts from meanings situated in the external described situation to meanings situated in the internal evaluative, perceptual, cognitive situation, and in the textual situation. Metonymy is largely correlated with shifts to meanings situated in the subjective belief-state or attitude toward the situation, including the linguistic one." The later stage of the course of grammaticalization is more abstract than the earlier stage (Lehman 1995[1982]). According to Heine *et al.* (1991), 'metaphorical abstraction' underlies grammaticalization. This abstraction concerns how we understand and conceptualize the world around us. It serves to relate more abstract contents with more concrete contents across conceptual domains, where the latter forms the metaphorical vehicles for the former (Heine *et al.* 1991). Let us look at Table 16.

Table 16 lists some of the more common distinctions found in the literature on grammaticalization. The domain where metaphorical vehicles belong is called source domain, and the domain where topic belongs is called target domain. In the following sections, the concessive conjunctions will be explained with the grammaticalization principles and mechanisms surveyed thus far.

Table 16. Vehicle and Topic in Metaphorical Abstraction

| | VEHICLE | TOPIC |
|---|---|---|
| IDEATIONAL | Clearly delineated, compact<br>physical(visible, tangible, etc.)<br>thing-like objects<br>sociophysical interactions<br>process<br>space<br>individual<br>absolute or quantified magnitude<br>autonomous | fuzzy, diffuse<br>non-physical, mental<br>qualities<br>mental processes<br>state<br>time, cause, manner<br>mass, class, non-countable<br>relative magnitude<br>relational |
| TEXTUAL | "real world"<br>less discourse-based<br>referential<br>central participant<br>new<br>presentational<br>independent | "world of discourse"<br>more discourse-based, or "speaker-based"<br>non-referential<br>circumstantial participant<br>old<br>relational<br>context-dependent |
| INTERPERSONAL | expressive | non-expressive |

(Heine *et al.* 1991: 41)

## 6.4 Concomitance of Circumstance: *though, although, even though*

*Though*, *although*, and *even though* are the concessive conjunctions developed from concomitance of circumstance, or case. In particular, *though* was at the root of the evolution of *although* and *even though*. *Though* has also developed into a discourse marker. According to Traugott (1992: 258-259), concessive clauses are of great complexity semantically and pragmatically. However, she claims that it is relatively straightforward syntactically. The prototypical marker of concession in OE is the conjunction *þeah* (*þe*). The example (102) is as quoted in Traugott (1992: 258-259). According to Traugott (1992: 259), concessives of this type typically take the subjunctive in the 'although'-clause, even though the factuality of the concessive clause is asserted.

(102) & ***þeah*** þæt folc nolde ær Gode abugan,
and although that people not-wanted earlier to-God obey,

hy hwæðre þa hyra unðances him gehyrsume wæron
they nevertheless then at-their unwillingness to-him obedient were
(Or 1 7.38.17)

'and although that people had not wanted to obey God earlier,
they then were nevertheless against their will obedient to him.'

Fischer (1992: 285) states that in OE, it is not always clear whether a conjunctive element functions as an adverb or a conjunction in any given clause, and consequently whether that clause is used dependently or independently. In many cases, however, according to Fischer (1992: 285-286), word order and/or the use of the subordinating particle *þe* help to decide the matter. In Early Middle English some of this OE 'vagueness' is still present, e.g. in the use of correlative constructions, but this is rapidly replaced by a more transparent system, in which conjunctions are distinct from adverbs according to Fischer (1992: 286). *Though/þeih/þah* can still function as adverbs as well as conjunctions in early texts as quoted in Fischer (1992: 287):

(103) Ich wat ***þah*** to soðe þ[et] ich schal bituhen ham neomen deaðes wunde.

(*Ancr.* (Corp-C) 199.11-12)

'Yet I know for certain that among them I shall receive death's wound.'

(104) ***þah*** ich ȝeue poure al þ[et] ich hefde, ȝef ich nefde luue þerwið, to godd,...al were I spillet,

(*Ancr.* (Corp-C) 196.13-15)

'although I give to the poor all that I have—if I do not it out of love for God,...all would be in vain'

However, in Chaucer *though* has become almost exclusively a conjunction (Fischer 1992: 287). In the 16th century, *that* can be found at least with *after, as, because, before, beside(s), for, if, since, sith, though, (un)till, when* and *while* (Rissanen 1999). Rissanen (1999: 303-311) argues that *that* is common in the 16th century. In the course of the 17th century, however, its popularity decreases rapidly. The relationship between conditional and concessive clause types can be seen in the fact that, as in ME, the prototypical conditional conjunction *if* can be used in concessive clauses as in (105) and the prototypical concessive conjunction *though* in conditional clauses as in (106):

(105)

***If*** Spirites of their owne accorde woulde gladly tell vs many thinges: yet wee must not giue eare vunto them

(1572 R. H. tr. Lauater's *Of ghostes* 197 [OED. *if*, 4a])

(106)

***Though*** a sprete or an angell hath apered to him, let vs not stryve agaynst God.

(Tyndale *Acts of Apostles* 23.9)

The intensifying *all* plays an important role in the formation of concessive links. It is combined with *though* in ME, and by the end of the period it had lost most of its emphasizing force. It can be found throughout the ModE period according to Rissanen (1999: 310). In PDE, *though* has the function as a discourse marker. It is used textually and interpersonally. We summarize the historical development of *though*, as represented in Table 17.

Table 17. Diachronic Development of *Though*

| Stage I | Stage II | Stage III |
|---|---|---|
| Concessive/conditional | Concessive | Concessive<br>Discourse Marker |
| - Sentential adverb<br>- Conjunction accompanying *that* | - Conjunction without *that* | - Topic shifter & other interpersonal functions |

In summary, *though* had functioned as a sentential adverb or conjunction in OE, meaning concession or condition. It still accompanied *that* until ME. In the 17th century, the pleonastic *that* disappeared after *though*, and functioned as a concessive marker. In PDE, *though* serves as a discourse marker as well.

### 6.4.1 Syntactic and Semantic Changes of *though*

In this section, the semantic changes of *though* will be explored. That is, it will be shown how its source meaning goes through grammaticalization, and what changes emerge in the course of grammaticalization from the concessive marker *though* to conjunctions *although* and *even though*.

According to the OED, *though,* originated in *þéah* in OE, was one of its phonetic and orthographic variants, and OE *þéah* corresponds to Gothic *þau* + *h* '*in that case* + *also*'. In the U.S. the form *tho* had been employed informally as an abbreviation of the word as indicated in the OED (Lee 2010: 306) in (107).

(107)

The committee now present the following words as the beginning of such [a] list [of reformed spellings], and recommend them for immediate use:.. Tho. Thru. Wisht.

(1879 *Proc. Amer. Philo. Assoc.* 6)

According to Lee (2010: 306), "*though* is an adversative particle expressing the relation of two opposed facts or circumstances (actual or hypothetical) in which the one is inadequate to prevent the other". Accordingly, both concur, contrary to what might be expected (OED). When used as an adverb, it is usually as an enclitic, as in 'he did though' (OED). For this example, *though* is employed as a discourse marker.

As mentioned above, *though* is associated with the Gothic *þauh* 'in that case also.' First, let us take into account the sense of *þauh* 'in that case also'. *Case* implies 'an instance or example of the occurrence or existence of a thing, fact, circumstance, etc' (Lee 2010: 306).

The important part which people use *though* as a concessive is *h* 'also' (Chen, 2000). The concomitant situation was admitted with *h*. The particle *h* 'also' in *þauh* 'in that case also' accomplishes the meaning of conceding the fact. Crosslinguistically, 'additive focus particles' like the English *also* and *too* are frequently a component of a concessive connective (König 1985). Because of *þau* 'in that case' and *h* 'also' in its source meaning, *though* undergoes the path to being a concessive. As claimed in Bybee (2006), grammatical morphemes always occur in and derive their meaning from specific constructions. As for *though*, without all the sources such as *in that case* and *also*, the concessive meaning would not have been construed (Lee 2010: 307). Let us look at the following example:

(108) They are no kings, ***though*** they possess the crown.

(1701 De Foe *True-born Eng.* II. 314)

There are some contexts in which concomitance may be highly relevant and worthy of pointing out: One context where there is a general incompatibility between the two situations, i.e. where one situation does not normally co-occur with the other (Traugott and König 1991). Like the example in (108), the situations 'they possess the crown' and 'they are not kings' do not co-occur. People who own the crown should be kings as we generally anticipate. Nevertheless, there is a conceptual domain in which the speaker does not acknowledge that they are kings. That domain is predominant for the speaker. The fact that they have crowns is the end of the extreme. Therefore, even in the case that they have crowns although that is a fact, they are not kings in the speaker's conceptual domain. The speaker's epistemic judgement, which is subjective belief-state/attitude toward the situation, is employed. *Though* comes by 'Semantic-pragmatic Tendency I' (Traugott and König 1991).

In addition, *þeah* accompanied *þe* in OE. However, in the course of the 17th century, the use of *that* decreased. As *that* introducing a clause had disappeared, for *though* which has the source meaning of the case, the textual function was emphasized, which is 'Semantic-pragmatic Tendency II' (Traugott and König 1991).

### 6.4.2 Persistence

Some traces of the original lexical meanings tend to adhere to the grammaticalized form, and its lexical history may be reflected in constraints on its grammatical distribution, which is called 'Persistence' (Hopper 1991). Viewed from the endpoint of a discourse marker *though*, it exhibits persistence. *Though* is "an adversative particle expressing the relation of two incompatible facts or circumstances in which both concur, contrary to what might be expected" (Lee 2010: 310). The primary use of the discourse marker *though* is introducing a proposition that is 'contrary to expectation.'

As a softening marker to disagree with the previous speaker, the discourse marker *though* still exhibits the contrast between two opinions. In case of a topic shifter as well, the contrast relation holds between two (sub)topics. Therefore, the discourse marker *though* adheres to its original lexical meaning.

### 6.4.3 Divergence vs Layering

Divergence (Hopper 1991) may apply to cases where one and the same autonomous lexical item is grammaticalized in one context and does not become grammaticalized in the other (Lee 2010). Divergence took place in the course of grammaticalization of *though*. The relation can be represented as follows:

(109) *though* (concessive) → *though* (concessive)
→ *though* (discourse marker)
⇒ local divergence
→ *although* (concessive)
→ *even though* (concessive)

(Lee 2010: 311)

Let us first consider the differences among *though*, *although* and *even though*. First, *though* has a function of concessive conjunction as well as a discourse marker. The discourse marker *though* is derived from a concessive, which is the case of local divergence. In addition, *although* and *even though* are concessive markers, and propositions they introduce should be spelled out and are syntactically fixed. However, both *although* and *even though* were originated from *though* to highlight the meaning of *though*, but *although* in fact has lost the emphatic force (Lee 2010: 311).

Layering (Hopper 1991) is that within a broad functional domain, new layers are continually emerging. Grammaticalization of *though* to *although* and *even though* is associated with layering. Let us look at (110) as below:

(110)

In more or less weakened or modified sense, often nearly coinciding with *if*, but usually retaining some notion of opposition:

(a) After negative or interrogative phrases with *wonder, marvel, be sorry, care,* etc., where *if* or *that* is now substituted.

- I do not mervel ***though*** they are ful of Church sinke.

(1557 North *Gueuara's Diall* Pr. 295)

(b) In phrase. *as though*: *as if*; as would or might be the case if; so as to suggest the supposition that. (With verb in past subjunctive (also with ellipsis), or with inf. of purpose: cf. as if s.v. IF 8c.) In quot. 1297, with ellipsis of as (obs.). In quot. 1963, with verb in present indicative.

- I have reason to love him ***as though*** he was my own son.

(1794 Mrs. Radcliffe Myst. Udolpho lii)

(c) Simply. *If. supposing that*. Obs. rare.

- ***Though*** a sprete or an angell hath apered to hym, lett vs not stryue agaynst God. (1526 Tindale *Acts* xxiii. 9)

(OED, *though*. conj. 4)

According to the OED, from c.1200, *though* 'nearly coincided with *if'* (OED, *though*, conj.4). In those times, since *though* has two meanings of 'conditional and concession'—in the 16th century, *though* was employed simply to denote the sense of *if* in (110c), it was reinforced by *all* and *even* for concession (Lee 2010: 311). The first appearance of *although* in literature was in c.1325 according to the OED. At that time, *all* emphasized the supposition or concession, following or preceding *though*. *All though* which was originally more emphatic than *though* was by 1400 practically only a variant of it. However, *all* had lost its independent force, and the phrase was written as one word. It can be found throughout the ModE period.

*Even though* is the more emphatic form of *though*; the modifying *even* also expresses unexpectedness (Quirk *et al.* 1986). *Even though* is not used by Shakespeare nor in the Bible of 1611 (OED *though*. conj. 5b). The functional relation of *though, although,* and *even though* can be diagrammed as follows:

(111)

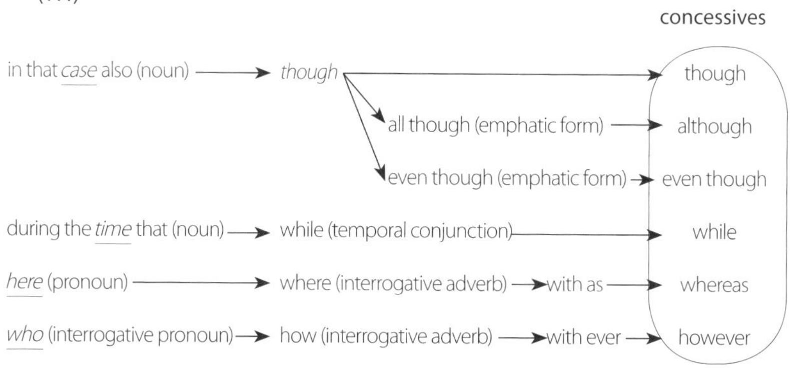


Layering (cf. Hopper 1991) is the evidence that language change cannot be explained in a teleological point-of-view (Rhee 1998). To correspond to a teleological point-of-view, speakers in that time would not have deployed both *though* and *although* when the latter was an equivalent of the former, not emphatic. Likewise, duc to the existence of concessive conjunctions such as *though*, *although*, and *even though*, both *whereas* in the early 16th century and *while* in the early 17th century would not have been employed as concessive in accordance with a teleological point-of-view (Lee 2010: 312).

### 6.4.4 *Though* in View of the Unidirectionality Hypothesis

Unidirectionality is a prominent hypothesis describing the processes of grammaticalization. This principle shows that language change comes about in multiple dimensional levels such as semantic, phonological, and syntactic levels; the changes occurring in multiple dimensions are unidirectional. The theory of unidirectionality may be summed up as follows:

semantic change: concrete meaning > abstract meaning

phonological change: independent element > dependent element

categorial/syntactic change: lexical item > grammatical item

(Rhee 1998: 193)

The creation of grammatical material as the evolution of substance from the more specific to the more general and abstract is consistent cross-linguistically (Bybee et al. 1994). However, the case of the development from *though* to *although* and *even though* is a counter-example of the Unidirectionality Hypothesis. In general, when there is one layer for a certain expression, that expression is renewed with a new form, which becomes another layer in the same functional domain. In case of *though*, however, the expression of the concessive *though* was repaired for the new layer; that is, the particles *all* and *even* are added to *though*.

The concession meaning of *though* got weakened. The speakers highlighted the salient concessive meaning of *though* by adding those particles, and as a result of that, the meaning is reinforced, not bleached. With the addition of particles, the phonetic volume is not eroded, but increased. Syntactically, one morphemic *though* became the two morphemic *all though* and *even though*, which is the opposite direction of the Unidirectionality Hypothesis. Univerbation took place from *all though* to *although*.

Accordingly, the grammaticalization from *though* to *although* and *even though* is a counter-example of the Unidirectionality Hypothesis semantically, phonetically, and syntactically. This reverse direction of change resulted because speakers chose to repair the existing form, not to renew the function with a totally different form.

## 6.5 Concomitance of Time: *while*

The concessive conjunction *while* is the one that was evolved from concomitance of time. *While* has the function of both temporal and concessive meaning. The following subsection shed light on the pathway of change from the noun *while* to the conjunction *while*.

*While* originated in OE in an adverbial phrase translatable as 'at the time that' consisting of the dative distal demonstrative, the dative noun *hwile* 'time,' and the subordinator *þe*, a highly explicit coding of simultaneity according to Traugott and König (1991). Traugott and König (1991: 200) provide an examples as below.

(112) & wicode þær þa ***hwile*** þe man þa burg worhte
and camped there that time that one that fortress worked-on
& getimbrede …
and built

(ChronA(Plummer)913.3)

'and camped there during the time that the fortress was built'

According to Traugott and König (1991: 201), this phrasal expression was reduced by late OE to the simple conjunction *wile* in (113).

(113) & ðæt lastede þa [xix] wintre ***wile*** Stephne was king

and that lasted those 19 winters while Stephen was king

(ChronE(Plummer)1137.36)

'and that went on for nineteen years while Stephen was king'

Traugott and König (1991: 201) claim that conditions specified in the subordinate clause serve not only as the temporal frame of reference for those in the main clause, but also as the grounds of the situation (the disasters lasted nineteen years because Stephen was king). They further argue that such an inference to grounds of the situation is dominant over temporality in the later 15th century and quote the instance of the coding of surprise and hence concessivity in the early 17th century.

(114) ***Whill*** others aime at greatnes boght with blod, Not to bee great thou stryves, bot to bee good.

(1617 Sir W. Mure Misc. Poems xxi.23)

'While others aim at greatness that is bought with blood, you strive to be not great but good.'

In (114), *while* is interpreted as a concessive. Temporal *while*, a textual marker, comes by Tendency III to express the speaker's surprise at the relation between two propositions (Traugott and König 1991: 209).

### 6.5.1 Decategorialization

*while* was used as a noun meaning 'period of time.' As a conjunction (late OE), it represents OE *þa hwile þe*; form *whiles* is recorded from early the 13th century. The development of *while* from a noun to a conjunction is related to decategorialization (cf. Hopper 1991).

Total hits of *while* as a noun are 5,899 cases in the BNC. We surveyed the top twenty collocations with *while* as a noun. To analyze the collocations, we surveyed the words, located to the third left from *while*. Except six different words demonstrated in Table 18, the other 14 words occur just one time each.

Table 18. Collocations of *While* as a Noun

| Word | Frequency |
|---|---|
| a | 5,059 |
| for | 3,082 |
| after | 827 |
| worth | 206 |
| short | 260 |
| little | 446 |

As Table 18 represents, as for collocations[8] with *while,* an indefinite article *a* among articles is accompanied, and the conjunction in question co-occurs with three prepositions *for*, *after*, and *worth*

8) As a result of surveying the website 'Google' the preposition *in* and the adjective *long* can be collocated with *while* as a noun. Still, the collocations are very limited.

among many, and with adjectives *short* and *little* among others. Because of this restrictions on the collocation it can be assumed that the noun *while* does not have the typical characteristics of nouns: features to be modified by various types of adjectives, to accompany definite or indefinite articles, and to function as objects of verbs (Lee 2014: 222).

This restricted usage of the noun *while* is attributed to the decategorialization (cf. Hopper 1991) of *while* as a conjunction. In other words, having lost the property of a noun, *while* gets the characteristics of a conjunction. This claim can be supported by the high frequency of conjunction *while*: 5,899 occurrences as a noun vs. 47,105 occurrences as a conjunction in the BNC (Lee 2014). In addition, since w*hile* was first used as a concessive conjunction in 16th century, it has been in the same functional category with concessive *though*, *although*, and *even though*.

### 6.5.2 Metaphor vs Metonymy

Rhee (2004: 5) discusses that the notion of semantic domains (Fillmore 1975, Langacker 1987, Lakoff 1987) is useful in both theory and practice for dealing with the meanings of words, as it enables categorization and comparisons with respect to similarities and differences. Such an act of categorizing things, both linguistic and non-linguistic, is believed to be deeply embedded in human perception and cognition. Rhee (2004: 5) claims, however, that since domains are thought to be dependent on and formed by experience, which is largely represented as image schematic, they cannot be either exhaustively listed or unambiguously delineated.

Rhee (2004: 4) further states that likewise, in a discussion of cognitive domains, Barcelona (2003: 230) notes that Langacker (1987: 154-158), Taylor (1995: 83-87), and most other cognitive linguists understand them as encyclopedic domains and, thus, that they will vary in breadth from person to person and may have no precise boundaries. For ease of explanation, we thus adopt frequently invoked terms in grammaticalization scholarship in this dissertation.

As for *while*, extension of the originally temporal noun to the concessive is operated by metaphoric transfer. Let us take a look at (115).

(115) a. White is vulgarly thought to be the most uncompounded of all Colours, ***while*** yet it really arises from a certain Proportion of the Seven primary Colours.

(1749 D. Hartley Observ. Man i. i. §2. 75)

b. ***While*** the object of the people was to free themselves from the yoke, the object of the nobles was merely to find new sources of excitement.

(1857 H. T. Buckle Hist. Civilisation Eng. I. x. 608)

The semantic transfer can occur from TIME to QUALITY (Heine *et al.* 1991). The contrastive events are not simple co-occurrences, but since one is foreground and the other is background, the one in the foreground is highlighted. Accordingly, notable contrastive meaning in temporal reference becomes a vehicle for the two contrastive propositions construed as concession. Contrast in temporal reference is unexpected and so is contrast in concessive meaning. This similarity between two domains in TIME and QUALITY gives rise to metaphor (Lee 2014).

Metonymic transfer also triggers semantic change. Stern (1968[1931]: 359) claims that permutations (his term for metonymy) results from "striving to fulfill as adequately as possible the symbolic and communicative functions of speech." He lists examples of permutation, one of which is the concessive *while.*

*While* was employed to imply concomitance of time. As indicated in (113)-(115), conditions introduced by *while* in the subordinate clause function as the temporal frame of reference for those in the main clause, and at the same time serve as the grounds of the situation (cf. Traugott and König 1991: 201). Such an inference to the grounds of the situation prevails over temporality and then *while* marks surprise and concessivity (cf. Traugott and König 1991: 201). Worth noticing that the meaning change from time via cause to concessivity is based on semantic contiguity.

## 6.6 Concomitance of Space: *whereas*

In English, the concessive conjunction derived from concomitance of space is *whereas*. *Whereas* consists of *where* and *as*. *Where* was derived from the interrogative stem χwa-, as *here* (OED). *As* is the worn-down form of *all-so*, OE *all-swá* 'wholly so, quite so, just so.' *Whereas*, in early use, was *where as* which originated in ME. In the subsections, the syntactic and semantic changes evolved in *whereas* will be illustrated.

### 6.6.1 Univerbation and Decategorialization

*Where* as a relative adverb and conjunctive adverb came to function as a conjunction with *as*. With many common adjectives and adverbs, *as* (*als*, etc.) was formerly written in combination, especially in idiomatic constructions, e.g. *asmuch*, *aswell*, *asfaste*, *assoon*, *astite*; relics of this survive in *forasmuch*, *inasmuch*, *whereas* according to the OED (cf. OED, *as*. adv.)

In early use from a.1375, *whereas* was used as the same meaning with *where*, which refers to 'physical position,' to 'at or to the point or stage of action, speech, etc.' in the passage, or to 'in the circumstances, position, or condition in which.' Later, from 1426-7, as an illative or adversative conjunction, *whereas* refers to 'in view or consideration of the fact that, seeing that, considering that, forasmuch as, inasmuch as' (OED). From 1535, *whereas* introduced a statement of fact in contrast or opposition to that expressed by the main clause (OED).

As Givón coined the memorable phrase "Today's morphology is yesterday's syntax" (Givón, 1971: 413), syntactic *where as* becomes a morphologic expression, *whereas*, which is one of univerbation (Lee 2014: 225). The spatial conjunction *whereas* was employed to indicate contrastive and adversative meaning in the 16th century, when *though* was already deployed as a concessive conjunction.

Since then, concessive *whereas* has co-existed and comprised layers with *though*, *although*, *even though*, and *while*.

### 6.6.2 Subjectification

In the pathways of grammaticalization of *whereas*, subjectification triggers the changes. *Whereas* originated in ME, as a relative adverb or as an adverbial phrase just like *where* as below.

(116) And quickly too he gat Unto the place ***whereas*** the Lady sat.

(1868 W. Morris Earthly Paradise ii. 655)

In (116), *whereas* modifies the antecedent *the place* as a relative adverb. From 1426, *Whereas* functioned as an illative or adversative conjunction. Let us look at (117).

(117) ***Where as*** it was thyne hert to buylde an house vnto my name, thou dyddest well, that thou wast so mynded.

(1539 Bible (Great) 1 Kings viii. 18)

'Because it was in your heart to build a temple for my Name, you did well to have this in your heart.'

In (117), *whereas* can be interpreted such as 'in view or consideration of the fact that.' The circumstance or condition specified in the subordinate clause functions as the grounds of result concluded in the main clause. For this reason, the relationship between a subordinate clause and a main clause in (117) can be connected with the marker denoting the causal relation in glossary. Semantic-pragmatic Tendency I (Traugott 1982, 1986, 1988, Traugott and König 1991) is associated with the meaning change from the physical position to that of circumstance or condition (Lee 2014: 227). Next, let us look at (118).

(118) Hee might haue worne the Diadem many yeares, ***whereas*** he bare the title of King no longer than two moneths.

(1631 J. Weever Anc. Funerall Monuments 520)

In (118), two situations in the subordinate and main clauses are contrasted in the cognitive space of the speaker (Lee 2014). *whereas* encodes unexpectedness of the situation in the main clause and hence the sense of concessivity is construed, which is related to Semantic-pragmatic Tendency III proposed by Traugott (1982, 1986, 1988).

### 6.6.3 Metaphor vs Metonomy

Metaphor is typically defined as a conceptual mechanism of understanding and experiencing one kind of thing in terms of another (Lakoff and Johnson 1980: 5). Heine *et al.* (1991) claim that there is unidirectionality in metaphorical mappings of tenor and vehicle as the following:

(119) PERSON 〉OBJECT 〉 PROCESS 〉 SPACE 〉TIME 〉QUALITY

Rhee (2004: 9) claims that in numerous works metaphor is a ubiquitous phenomenon (notably in research by Heine and his colleagues, and Lakoff and Johnson 1980). Metaphor triggers the semantic change in *whereas* (Lee 2014).

(120) a. And quickly too he gat Unto the place ***whereas*** the Lady sat.

(1868 W. Morris Earthly Paradise ii. 655)

b. *Whereas* he had received a very handsome Fortune with his Wife, he had now spent every penny of it.

(1749 H. Fielding Tom Jones IV. x. iii. 21)

In (120a), *whereas* refers tothe space (i.e. the SPACE domain in Heine *et al.* (1991)), and in (120b), it signifies concession. Concession is associated with validity of the speaker—it can be construed as the QUALITY domain in Heine *et al.* (1991). This change corresponds to a categorial metaphor (Heine *et al.* 1991) whereby a concept belonging to the domain of concrete items, i.e. SPACE domain, plays a role of a structural template to represent concepts belonging to the QUALITY domain (Lee 2014).

As indicated in Table 16, space is used as the metaphorical vehicle to express concepts of 'time, cause, manner' (Heine *et al.* 1991). "The similarity which triggers metaphoric transfer is 'contrast' in spatial references and in propositions, and the contrast is construed for concessive meaning" (Lee 2014: 228). "The implication of this conceptual transfer is that the relevant term for place loses properties to modify a noun associated with a place and increasingly acquires properties to link with the category of conjunctions" (Lee 2014: 228).

Semantic change of *whereas* is associated with metonymic change, i.e. the conceptual contiguity representable as from space (position) to circumstance (cause) and to concession (Lee 2014). Let us take a look at (121).

(121) a. Ornaments on that upright, *whereas* the Southerly windes raise much dust.

(1663 B. Gerbier Counsel to Builders 12)

b. ***Whereas*** the Emperour and the Catholicke Princes, by many Letters made intercession, that the displaced Bishops might be mercifully dealt withall· ·shee answered [etc.].

(1630 R. Norton tr. W. Camden Hist. Princesse Elizabeth i. 31)

c. I brought him up in ignorance of his father, whom he had always imagined to be a gentleman; ***whereas*** he was only a sergeant in a Line regiment.

(1882 W. Besant All Sorts of Men II. xxiv. 148)

Space or position in (121a) can be interpreted as the circumstance of the fact as (121b). The circumstance of the fact can be construed as grounds for the main clause, which is the causal chain (Lee 2014). Causal relation is related concept with concession, already discussed in the previous sections. Concessive meaning is formed with deflection of the causal chain on relative scales.

## 6.7 Concomitance of Manner: *however*

The last but not least concomitance source related with concessive conjunctions is manner. In English, *however* is represented as a concessive conjunction from concomitance of manner. The concessive conjunction *however* consists of *how*, an adverb, and *ever*, an adverb. Etymology of *how*[9] is OE *hú* (< *hwó), from W.Gmc. **khwo-* (cf. O.S. *hwo*, O.Fris., M.Du. *hu*, Du. *hoe*, Ger. *wie*, Goth. *hvaiwa* "how"), from common PIE interrogative pronominal stem. In subsections, the changes with respect to *however* will be illustrated in terms of grammaticalization.

### 6.7.1 Univerbation and Decategorialization

Etymology of *however how* and *ever* as just mentioned. *How* is an adverb primarily interrogative, used also in exclamations, and in conjunctive and relative constructions (OED). *How* qualifies a verb meaning "in what way or manner" (OED) or qualifies an adjective or adverb meaning "to what extend, in what degree (that), adjective *however*" (OED). In phrases, *how* means "however much" equivalent to *notwithstanding that* or *although*, but it is obsolete (OED).

The adverb *ever* means "on any supposition, by any chance, or at all" (OED). Following interrogative pronouns and adverbs, *ever* intimates that the speaker has no notion what the answer will be (OED, *ever.* adv. 8d).

---

9) Look at the website ***www.etymonline.com*** for etymology mentioned.

*How* and *ever* became a single word, so-called univerbation. Univerbation includes the uniting of the two parts of a compound into a single lexical item (Hopper and Traugott 2003[1993]: 145). Whereas the ancestral independent word may have had a certain amount of positional freedom, univerbation removes any flexibility of position. (Hopper and Traugott 2003[1993]: 148). In case of *however*, unlike two adverbs *how* and *ever*, the position of *however* as the conjunction is fixed, introducing the clause, as show in (122). *However* from an adverb came to introduce a subordinate clause, leading to decategorizalization (cf. Hopper 1991).

(122) a. The Troll began to wonder..***how ever*** they could be rid of the lad.

(1859 G.W. DASENT *Pop. Tales from Norse* 163)

b. The Idea of Black is no less positive in his Mind, than that of White, ***however*** the cause of that Colour in the external Object, may be only a Privation.

(J. LOCKE Ess. *Humane Understanding* II. viii. 55)

### 6.7.2 Metaphor versus Metonymy

Discussing the ontological categories PERSON-OBJECT-PROCESS-SPACE-TIME-QUALITY, Heine *et al.* (1991: 49) state that the category QUALITY is the most fuzzy of all of these entities and it forms a kind of catchall for a number of quite divergent conceptualizations as in Table 19. They further claim that one area where the categories distinguished above perhaps most clearly reflected in language structure is that of pronouns, and that interrogative pronouns tend to be structured lexically in a way that largely mirrors these categories (Heine *et al.* 1991: 55).

Table 19. Conceptual Categories and Pronominal Meaning

| Category | Pronominal Meaning |
|---|---|
| PERSON | 'who?' |
| OBJECT/ACTIVITY | 'what?' |
| SPACE | 'where?' |
| TIME | 'when?' |
| QUALITY/MANNER | 'how?' |

(Heine *et al.* 1991: 58)

While it remains unclear what the exact correlations between the linguistic and the cognitive structure of pronouns are, a few assumptions may be tentatively formulated (Heine *et al.* 1991: 58). First, the relative degree of morphological complexity that a pronoun exhibits is likely to correlate to some extent which is the relative degree of its cognitive complexity (Heine *et al.* 1991: 58). This is in line with the "complexity principle" proposed by Clark (1978: 230), according to which "complexity in thought tends to be reflected in complexity of expression." They exemplify an interrogative pronoun that is expressed cross-linguistically by means of bimorphemic form that is likely to be conceptually more complex than one that is expressed by one morpheme only.

Second, formal similarity between different pronominal categories may be indicative of some kind of conceptual relation between these categories (Heine *et al.* 1991: 58). Heine *et al.* (1991: 58) furthermore discuss interrogative pronouns referring to the categories PERSON, OBJECT/ACTIVITY, SPACE, TIME, and QUALITY exhibit the least degree of morphological complexity and are clearly distinguished in all languages studies. According to Heine *et al.* (1991: 59), this may suggest that the metaphorical categories figuring in grammaticalization process in general are in fact salient taxa of the conceptual universe.

As explained in Heine et al (1991: 58), *how*, one component of *however*, is an adverbial formation of the interrogative pronoun and means 'manner.' Thus, the source meaning of *however* belongs to QUALITY of the metaphorical categories. The target meaning of *however* is concession, which is more abstract because concession correlate to the speakers' epistemic judgement toward two events. As for *however*, the source domain and the target domain both belong to QUALITY.

Notwithstanding Heine *et al.* (1991)' refined explanation on the ontological categories, the reason that this kind of problem arises is that the metaphorical categories are somewhat extensive. The domain change is the main characteristics of metaphor. Since there is no domain change in reference to *however*, metaphor alone is not the appropriate mechanism even though intuitively the change of *however* is by metaphor; rather, metonymy is a suitable mechanism to explain the meaning change with metaphor. This approach is in line with Goossen's observation that, "although metonymy and metaphor are clearly distinct in principle, they are not always separable in practice" (1989: 19). Derived from manner, *however* as a concessive conjunction forms parts of a more abstract conceptualization, based on contiguity.

## 6.8 Different Consequences in accordance with Sources

The notion of concessivity is closely related to unexpectedness and surprise. The concessive conjunctions from the nominal origins were derived from the sources of the concomitance: circumstance, time, space, and manner. The strategy that speakers employ to convey concessive meaning in these cases is to select two conceptual entities that are normally incompatible; thus, placing them juxtaposed would make them unexpected and noteworthy. The creation of the sense of noteworthiness in an unprepared mind may be achieved by a variety of means, but the most effective way is to bring in an entity that seems to be unsignificante or irrelevant or even contradictory. "When such an entity is brought into the scene, it may, at first, serve as a background of the proposition that is being foregrounded and asserted" (Lee 2014: 229). A natural human propensity is to "elicit meaningfulness from any co-occurring entities, a cognitive process that often results in attribution of contrastiveness" (Lee 2014: 230). Undoubtedly, the contrastive relation is closely associated with unexpectedness.

Unexpected information to speakers is linguistically marked with a grammatical marker that carries the function of 'mirative' (cf. DeLancey 2001). Mirativitiy, in other words, implies that the information represents knowledge which is new to the speaker, or knowledge which is already interpreted into the speaker's picture of the world (DeLancey 2001: 379).

Let us consider the nominal origin concessive conjunctions. As for *though*, *although*, and *even though*, they all have source meaning of co-occurrences of case. On the other hand, *while*, *whereas*, and *however* were evolved from sources of co-occurrences of time, space, and manner respectively. Coexisted propositions give rise to the contrastive relation, for one of the two propositions is more focused, so contrastive relation is closely assiciated with mirativity (Lee 2014: 230). *Though*, *although*, *even though*, *while*, *whereas*, and *however* mark concessivity. To summarize our discussion, we present Figure 15 illustrating the development paths leading to concessive grams.

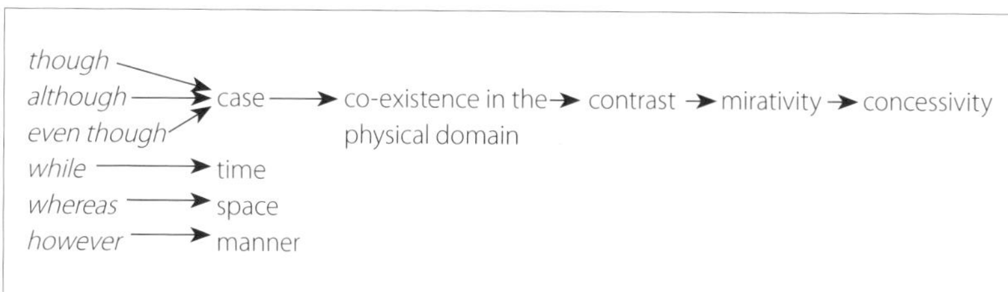

Figure 15. Paths of Development Leading to Concessivity

The grammaticalization pathways of the concessive conjunctions such as *though, although, even though, whereas,* and *while* are associated with the source determination hypothesis (Bybee *et al.* 1994). According to Bybee *et al.* (1994: 9), "the actual meaning of the construction that enters into grammaticalization uniquely determines the path that grammaticalization follows and, consequently, the resulting grammatical meaning." For instance, the motion verbs *come* and *go,* the dynamic transitive verb *do,* and the stative verbs *have* and *be* are selected most often for grammaticalization (Bybee *et al.* 1994: 9). All verbs adduced represent the basic semantic features of their domains.

The semantic developments from nominal origins to concession are good examples of a close relationship between the source and target meanings by which new designations for a given concept go back to conceptually similar sources. As shown in Figure 15 above, *though*, *although*, *even though*, *while*, *whereas*, and *however* have undergone the similar semantic extension [coexistence> contrast> mirativity> concession] (see Lee, 2014).

This similarity between the semantic changes of the concessive conjunctions from nominal origins lies in the source determination hypothesis (Bybee *et al.* 1994). In other words, the same source meanings of 'concomitance' seem to have triggered a similar semantic evolution (Lee 2014).

As indicated in Figure 16, the source nouns of *though*, *while*, *whereas*, and *however* in an adverbial phrases were analyzed as a conjunction. *Although* and *even though* had emerged to emphasize concessivity of *though* as a conjunction. *Though* and *while* in an adverbial phrase accompanied *that.* However, in the course of grammaticalization, the pleontic *that* was deleted and *though* and *while* took over the clauses. While there is an exception of *even though*, the nominal origin concessive conjunctions composing of another factor underwent morpho-syntactic reduction as indicated in (123):

(123) *all though* → *although*
*where as* → *whereas*
*how ever* → *however*

As indicated in (123) and in the dotted box in Figure 16, in the course of diachronic development, univerbation took place. In sum, the concessive conjunctions from nominal origins all experienced the complex phrasal stages, reanalyzed, and became single words, except *even though*, where another component was added.

Although concessive conjunctions are derived from the similar sources of concomittance, conjunctions from case, time, space, and manner respectively show difference in frequency of use. Among these concessives with nominal origins, *while*, *whereas*, and *however,* which are derived from 'time, space, and manner' are younger, i.e. grammaticalized later than *though*, *although*, and *even though* derived from 'case'.

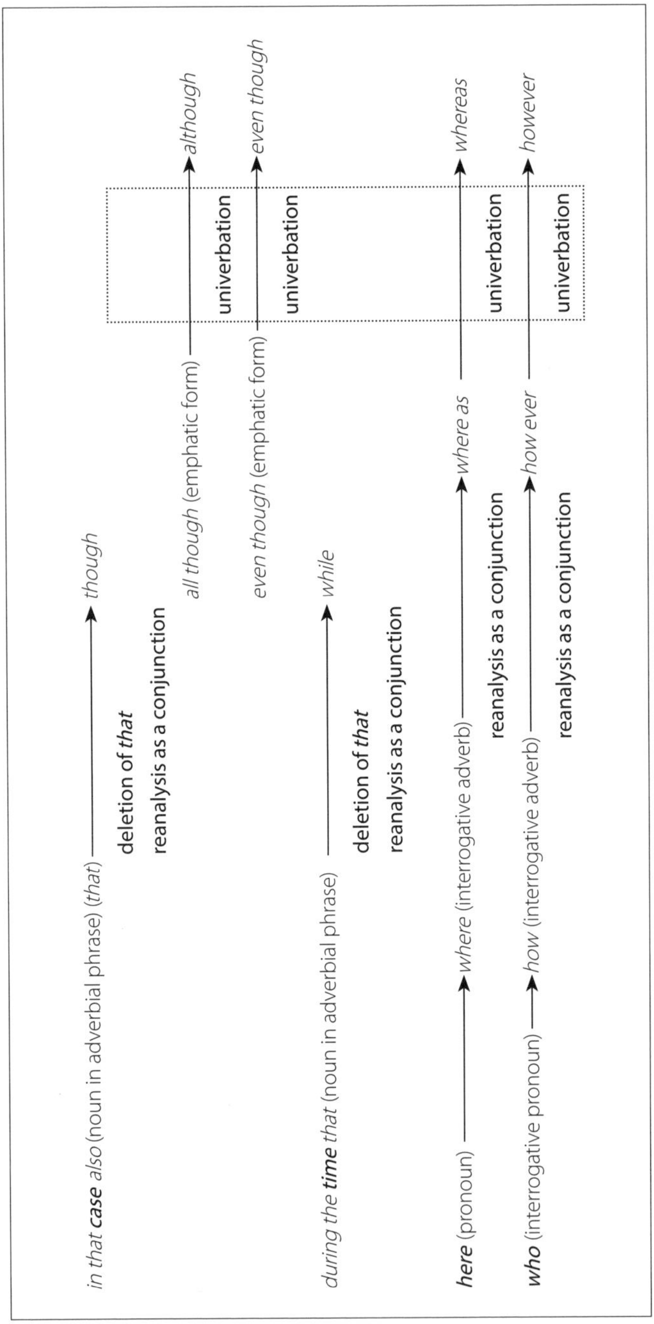


Figure 16. The Morpho-Syntactic Change of the Concessive Conjunctions Derived from Nominal Origins

As represented in Table 20, the concessive conjunctions such as *though*, *although*, and *even though* with the source of concomitance of case have 69,999 occurrences, ranked with the highest frequency. Concessive conjunctions in the intermediate stage, i.e. younger grams, derived from concomitance of time, space, and manner, have 44,204 occurrences.

Table 20. The Frequency of Concessives in the Written Domain by Sources

| Categorial Distinction | Nominal Origins | | | |
|---|---|---|---|---|
| Source Meaning | Case | Time | Space | Manner |
| Total Frequency | 69,999 | 33,912 | 5,504 | 4,788 |

In terms of textual domains, *though* is used a lot in 'Imaginary prose' while *although* is dominant in scientific texts. This difference preference is interpreted as style, that is, informal or formal. The concessive conjunction *while* occurs with the highest frequency in the 'World affairs' domain. *Whereas* is specialized chiefly in legal or other formal documents. *Whereas* takes over one of the functions *where* had been used before. This restriction in use can be interpreted as 'persistence' (cf. Hopper 1991). In addition, the use in the special genre 'Social science' is attributed to its 'specialization' (cf. Hopper 1991). Because of a preference for *whereas* in legal contexts, its total frequency is relatively low. *However* occurs with the lowest frequency among concessive conjunctions derived from nominal origins due to of a preference for *however* as an adverb.

# Bibliography

Aarts, Bas. 1988. Clauses of concession in written present-day British English. *Journal of English Linguistics* 21, 39-58.

Ahn, Mikyung. 2009. *Emergence of Causality in Grammar: Causal Complex Prepositions in English.* Seoul: Hankookmunhwasa.

Altenberg, Bengt. 1986. Contrastive linking in spoken and written English. In Gunnel Tottie and Ingegerd Backlund (eds.), *English in speech and writing. A symposium,* 13-40. (Acta Universitatis Updsliensis, Studia Anglistica Upsaliensis 60). Uppsala, Stockholm: Almquist and Wiksell.

Antaki, Charles and Magaret Wetherell. 1999. Show concessions. *Discourse Studies* 1, 7-27.

Anttila, Raimo. 1972. An introduction to deductive change. *Language* 49, 765-793.

Ariel, Mira and John W. Du Bois. 2010. Concession and contrast: *Though* and *but* at the Intonation Unit boundary. Paper presented at Language, Interaction, and Social Organization, October 1, 2010, University of California, Santa Barbara.

Azar, Moshe. 1997. Concessive relations as argumentation. *Text* 17.3, 301-316.

Barcelona, Antonio. 2003. Metonymy in cognitive linguistics: An analysis and a few modest proposals. In Hubert Cuyckens, Thomas Berg, René Dirven, and Klaus-Uwe Panther (eds.), *Motivations in Language*, 223-255. Amsterdam & Philadelphia: John Benjamins.

Barth, Dagmar. 2000. That's true, although not really, but still: Expressing concession in spoken English. In Elizabeth Couper-Kuhlen and Bernd Kortmann (eds.), *Cause, Condition, Concession, Contrast: Cognitive and Discourse Perspectives*, 411-437. Berlin & New York: Mouton de Gruyter.

Barth-Weingarten, Dagmar and Elizabeth Couper-Kuhlen. 2002. On the development of final *though*: A case of grammaticalization? In Ilse Wischer and Gabriele Diewald (eds.), *New Reflections on Grammaticalization,* 345-361. Amsterdam & Philadelphia: John Benjamins.

Beaman, Karen. 1984. Coordination and subordination revisited: Syntactic complexity in spoken and written narrative discourse. In Deborah Tannen (ed.), *Coherence in Spoken and Written Discourse,* 45-80. Norwood & New Jersey: Ablex.

Biber, Douglas, Susan Conrad, and Randi Reppen. 1998. *Corpus Linguistics: Investigating Language Structure and Use*. Cambridge: Cambridge University Press.

Blake, Norman F. 1992. Translation and the history of English. In Matti Rissanen, Ossi Ihalainen, Terttu Nevalainen, and Irma Taavitsainen (eds.), *History of Englishes: New Methods and Interpretations in Historical Linguistics*, 3-24. Berlin & New York: Mouton de Gruyter.

Blakemore, Diane. 1987. *Semantic Constraints on Relevance*. Oxford: Blackwell.

Blakemore, Diane. 2000. Indicators and procedures: *Nevertheless* and *but*. *Journal of Linguistics* 36, 463-486.

Blakemore, Diane. 2002. *Relevance and Linguistic Meaning: The Semantics and Pragmatics of Discourse Markers*. Cambridge: CUP.

Brinton, Laurel J. 1996. *Pragmatic Markers in English: Grammaticalization and Discourse Functions*. Berlin: Mouton de Gruyter.

Brown, Gillian. 1977. *Listening to Spoken English*. London: Longman.

Burnard, Lou. 2007[2000]. *Reference Guide for the British National Corpus* (XML Edition). Online, available at: http://www.natcorp.ox.ac.uk/docs/URG/

Bybee, Joan L. 2006. *Frequency of Use and the Organization of Language*. New York: Oxford University Press.

Bybee, Joan L., Revere Perkins, and William Pagliuca. 1994. *The Evolution of Grammar: Tense, Aspect, and Modality in the Languages of the World*. Chicago & London: The University of Chicago Press.

Chafe, Wallace. 1984. How people use adverbial clauses. *Berkeley Linguistics Society* 10, 437-449.

Chen, Guohua. 2000. The grammaticalization of concessive markers in Early Modern English. In Olga Fischer, Anette Rosenbach, and Dieter Stein (eds.), *Pathways of Change*:

*Grammaticalization in English,* 85-110. Amsterdam: John Benjamins.

Clark, Eve V. and Herbert H. Clark. 1978. Universals, relativity, and language processing. In Joseph H. Greenberg, Charles A. Ferguson, and Edith A. Moravcsik (eds.), *Universals of Human Language* 4 vols. Vol. 1, 225-277. California: Stanford University Press.

Claudi, Ulrike and Bernd Heine. 1986. On the metaphorical base of grammar. *Studies in Language* 10.2, 297-335.

Couper-Kuhlen, Elizabeth and Sandra A. Thompson. 2000. Concessive patterns in conversation. In Elizabeth Couper-Kuhlen and Bernd Kortmann (eds.), *Cause, Condition, Concession, Contrast*: *Cognitive and Discourse Perspectives*, 381-410. Berlin & New York: Mouton de Gruyter.

Crevels, Mily 2000. *Concession*: *A Typological Study.* Ph.D. Dissertation, University of Amsterdam.

Crevels, Mily 2000. Concessives on different semantic levels. In Elizabeth Couper-Kuhlen and Bernd Kortmann (eds.), *Cause, Condition, Concession, Contrast*: *Cognitive and Discourse Perspectives*, 313-339. Berlin & New York: Mouton de Gruyter.

DeLancey, Scott. 2001. The mirative and evidentiality. *Journal of Pragmatics* 33, 369-382.

Diessel, Holger. 2001. The ordering distribution of main and adverbial clauses: A typological study. *Language* 77, 345-365.

Du Bois, John W. 2007. The stance triangle. In Robert Englebretson (ed.), *Stancetaking in Discourse: Subjectivity, Evaluation, Interaction*, 139-182. Amsterdam: John Benjamins.

Edda Weigand and Marcelo Dascal. 2001. *Negotiation and Power in Dialogic Interaction.* John Benjamins Publishing

Fauconnier, Gilles. 1994. *Mental spaces.* Cambridge: Cambridge University Press. First published in 1985 by MIT Press.

Fillmore, Charles J. 1975. An alternative to checklist theories of meaning. *Berkeley Linguistics Society* 1, 123-132.

Fischer, Olga. 1992. Syntax. In Norman F. Blake (ed.), *The Cambridge History of The English Language* 4 vols. Vol. 2, 207-408. Cambridge & New York: Cambridge University Press.

Ford, Cecilia. 1993. *Grammar in Interaction: Adverbial Clauses in American English Conversations*. Cambridge: Cambridge University Press.

Fraser, Bruce. 1988. Types of English discourse markers. *Acta Linguistica Hungarica* 38, 19-33.

Fraser, Bruce. 1990. An approach to discourse markers. *Journal of Pragmatics* 14, 383-395.

Fraser, Bruce. 1999. What are discourse markers? *Journal of Pragmatics*, 31, 931-952.

Fuller, Janet M. 2003. The influence of speaker roles on discourse marker use. *Journal of Pragmatics* 35, 23-45.

Gamillscheg, Ernst. 1957. *Historische Französische Syntax*. Tübingen: Max Niemeyer.

Givón, Talmy. 1971. Historical syntax and synchronic morphology:

An archaeologist's field trip. *Chicago Linguistic Society* 7, 394-415.

Goossens, Louis. 1989. *Metonymy in Metaphorization: From Body Parts (and Other Donor Domains) to Linguistic Action.* Duisburg: Universität Duisburg.

Greenbaum, Sidney. 1969. *Studies in English Adverbial Usage.* London: Longman.

Grice, H. Paul 1975. Logic and conversation. In Peter Cole and Jerry Morgan (eds.), *Syntax and Semantics.* Vol. 3, 41-58. New York: Academic Press.

Grober, Ellen H., William Beardsley and Alfonso Caramazza. 1978. Parallel function strategy in pronoun assignment. *Cognition* 6, 117-133.

Grote, Brigitte, Nils Lenke and Manfred Stede. 1997. Marking concessions in English and German. *Discourse Processes* 24, 87-117.

Heine, Bernd. 1991. The Hausa particle *nàa*. In Daniela Mendel and Ulrike Claudi (eds.), *Ägypten im afro-orientalischen Kontext: Aufsätze zur Archäologie, Sprache und Geschichte eines unbegrenzten Raumes*, 157-170. (AAP-Afrikanistische Arbeitspapiere, Sondernummer 1991) Gedenkschrift Peter Behrens.

Heine, Bernd. 1997. *Cognitive Foundations of Grammar.* New York & Oxford: Oxford University Press.

Heine, Bernd and Mechthild Reh. 1984. *Grammaticalization and Reanalysis in African Languages.* Hamburg: Helmut Buske.

Heine, Bernd, Ulrike Claudi, and Friederike Hünnemeyer. 1991. *Grammaticalization: A Conceptual Framework.* Chicago & London: The University of Chicago Press.

Heine, Bernd, Tom Güldemann, Christa Kilian-Hatz, Donald A. Lessau, Heinz Roberg, Mathias Schldadt, and Thomas Stolz. 1993. *Conceptual Shift: A Lexicon of Grammaticalization Processes in African Languages.* Köln: Afrikanistische Arbeitspapiere.

Hermodsson, Lars. 1978. *Semantische Strukturen der Satzgefüge im kausalen und konditionalen Bereich.* Uppsala: Almqvist and Wiksell.

Hermodsson, Lars. 1994. Der Begriff *konzessiv*: Terminologie und analysen. *Studia Neophilologica* 45, 298-305.

Hoffmann, Sebastian. 2005. *Grammaticalization and English Complex Prepositions: A Corpus-based Study.* London & New York: Routledge.

Hopper, Paul J. 1986. Some discourse functions of classifiers in Malay. In Colette Craig (ed.), *Noun Classes and Categorization*, 309-325. Amsterdam: John Benjamins.

Hopper, Paul J. 1991. On some principles of grammaticization. In Elizabeth C. Traugott and Bernd Heine (eds.), *Approaches to Grammaticalization*, 2 vols. Vol. 1, 17-35. Amsterdam: John Benjamins.

Hopper, Paul J. and Elizabeth C. Traugott. 2003[1993]. *Grammaticalizaiton.* 2nd ed. Cambridge: Cambridge University Press.

Izutsu, Mitsuko Narita. 2007. Contrast, concessive, and corrective: Toward a comprehensive study of opposition relations. *Journal of Pragmatics* 40, 646-675.

Jakobson, Roman and Morris Halle. 2002[1956]. *Fundamentals of Language*. Berlin & New York: Mouton de Gruyter.

Jordan, Michael P. 1998. The power of negation in English: Text, context and relevance. *Journal of Pragmatics*, 705-752.

Keller, Eric. 1979. Gambits: Conversational strategy signals. *Journal of Pragmatics* 3, 219-238.

Kiparsky, Paul. 1968. Linguistic universals and linguistic change. In Emmon Bach and Robert T. Harms (eds.), *Universals in Linguistic Theory*, 171-202. New York: Oxford University Press.

Kjellmer, Göran. 1989. *Even if* and *even though*. *English Studies* 3, 256-269.

König, Ekkehard. 1985. On the history of concessive connectives in English: Diachronic and synchronic evidence. *Lingua* 66, 1-19.

König, Ekkehard. 1986. Conditionals, concessive conditionals and concessives: Areas of contrast, overlap and neutralization. In Elizabeth C. Traugott, Alice ter Meulen, Judy Reilly and Charles A. Ferguson (eds.), *On Conditionals*, 229-246. Cambridge: Cambridge University Press.

König, Ekkehard. 1988. Concessive connectives and concessive sentences: Cross-linguistic regularities and pragmatic principles. In John A. Hawkins (ed.), *Explaining Language*

*Universals*, 145-166. New York: Blackwell.

König, Ekkehard. 1991. Concessive relations as the dual of causal relations. In Dietmar Zaefferer (ed.), *Semantic Universals and Universal Semantics*, 190-209. Dordrecht: Foris.

König, Ekkehard. 1994. Concessive clauses. In Robert E. Asher (ed.), *The Encyclopedia of Language and Linguistics,* 679-681. Oxford: Pergamon Press.

König, Ekkehard and Peter Siemund. 2000. Causal and concessive clauses: Formal and semantic relations. In Elizabeth Couper-Kuhlen and Bernd Kortmann (eds.), *Cause, Condition, Concession and Contrast*: *Cognitive and Discourse Perspectives*, 341-360. Berlin & New York: Mouton de Gruyter.

Koo, Hyun Jung and Seongha Rhee. 2008. Manipulated hypotheticality in conditionals: A journey in search of strength and diversity. Paper presented at the 4th New Reflections on Grammaticalization, July 16-19, 2008, Catholic University of Leuven.

Kortmann, Bernd. 1997. *Adverbial Subordination*: *A Typology and History of Adverbial Subordinators Based on European Languages.* (EALT 18.) Berlin/New York: Mouton de Gruyter.

Kövecses, Zoltán and Günter Radden. 1998. Metonymy: Developing a cognitive linguistic view. *Cognitive Linguistics* 9, 37-77.

Lakoff, George. 1987. *Women, Fire, and Dangerous Things*: *What Categories Reveal about the Mind.* Chicago & London: The

University of Chicago Press.

Lakoff, George and Mark Johnson. 1980. *Metaphors We Live By*. Chicago: The University of Chicago Press.

Langacker, Ronald. 1987. *Foundations of Cognitive Grammar*. Stanford: Stanford University Press.

Lee, Hyun Sook. 2010. Grammaticalization of *though* in English. *Studies in Modern Grammar* 62, 295-315.

Lee, Hyun Sook. 2010. *Grammaticalization of Concessive Markers in English from Verbal and Nominal Sources*. Ph. D. Dissertation, Hankuk University of Foreign Studies.

Lee, Hyun Sook. 2014. How does co-existence in the mental and physical domain go for concessives? *The Journal of Linguistic Science* 71, 217-236.

Lehmann, Christian. 1995[1982]. *Thoughts on Grammaticalization*. München & Newcastle: Lincom Europa.

Lenk, Uta. 1998. Discourse Markers and Global Coherence in Conversation. *Journal of Pragmatics* 30.2, 245-257.

Levinson, Stephen. 1983. *Pragmatics*. Cambridge: Cambridge University Press.

Lord, Carol. 1982. The development of object markers in serial verb languages. In Paul J. Hopper and Sandra A. Thompson (eds.), *Studies in Transitivity*, 277-300. London: Academic Press.

Lühr, Rosemarie. 1984. Reste der athematischen Konjugation in den germanischen Sprachen. In Jürgen Untermann and Bela Brogyani (eds.), *Das Germanische und die Rekonstruktion der indogermanischen Grundsprache*, 29-90. Amsterdam: John Benjamins.

Lyons, John. 1995. *Linguistic Semantics: An Introduction.* Cambridge: Cambridge University Press.

Mann, William C. and Sandra A. Thompson. 1986. Relational propositions in discourse. *Discourse Processes* 9, 57-90.

Mann, William C. and Sandra A. Thompson. 1988. Rhetorical structure theory: Towards a functional theory of text organization. *Text* 8.3, 243-281.

Mann, William C. and Sandra A. Thompson. 1992. Relational discourse structure: A comparison of approaches to structuring text by 'contrast'. In Shin Ja Hwang and William R. Merrifield (eds.), *Language in Context: Essays for Robert E. Longacre,* 19-45. Dallas: SIL.

Martin, James Robert. 1992. *English Text: System and Structure.* Amsterdam: Benjamins.

Matthiessen, Christian. 1995. *Lexicogrammatical cartography: English systems.* Tokyo: International Language Sciences Publishers

McEnery, Tony and Andrew Wilson. 2001[1996]. *Corpus Linguistics*. Edinburgh: Edinburgh University Press.

Meillet, Antonie. 1958[1912]. L'èvolution des formes grammaticales. *Linguistique Historique et Linguistique Générale*, 130-148. Paris: Edouard Champion.

Mulkay, Michael. 1985. Agreement and disagreement in conversation and letters. *Text 5*, 201-227.

Mustanoja, Tauno. 1960. *A Middle English Syntax*. Helsinki: Société Néophilologique.

Ochs, Elinor. 1979. Planned and unplanned discourse. In Talmy Givon (ed.), *Syntax and semantics*, Vol.12(4), 51-80. Sanfrancisco: Academic Press.

Ono, Tsuyoshi and Sandra A. Thompson. 1996. Interaction and syntax in the structure of conversational discourse. In Eduard Hovy and Donia Scott (eds.), *Discourse Processing: An Interdisciplinary Perspective*, 67-96. Heidelberg: Springer-Verlag.

Pomerantz, Anita. 1984. Agreeing and disagreeing with assessments: some features of preferred/dispreferred turn shapes. In J. Maxwell Atkinson and John Heritage (eds.), *Structures of Social Action: Studies in Conversation Analysis,* 57-101. Cambridge: Cambridge University Press.

Quirk, Randolph, Sidney Greenbaum, Geoffrey Leech, and Jan Svartvik. 1985. *A Comprehensive Grammar of the English Language*. London: Longman.

(*The*) *Oxford English Dictionary*. *http://dictionary.oed.com*.

Redeker, Gisela. 1990. Ideational and pragmatic markers of discourse structure. *Journal of Pragmatics* 14, 367-381.

Reinhardt, Mechthild. 1997. Some notes on concessive *but*. In Mechthild Reinhardt and Wolfgang Thiele (eds.), *Grammar and Text in Synchrony and Diachrony: In Honor of Gottfried Graustein,* 233-244. Frankfurt/Main: Verlag Iberoamericana.

Rhee, Seongha. 1998. *Mwunpephwauy Ihay* [Understanding

Grammaticalization]. Seoul: Hankuk Publisher.

Rhee, Seongha. 2004. Semantic structure of English prepositions: An analysis from a grammaticalizatin perspective. *Language Research* 40.2, 397-427.

Rhee, Seongha. 2005. Variability of formal reduction in Grammaticalization. *The Journal of Linguistic Science* 32, 251-268.

Rissanen, Matti. 1999. Syntax. In Roger Lass (ed.), *The Cambridge History of The English Language* 4 vols. Vol. 3, 187-331. Cambridge & New York: Cambridge University Press.

Rousan, Rafat M Al. The Use of Discourse Marker "MAʕ NAFSAK" in Saudi Arabic: A pragmatic Perspective. *International Journal of Linguistics* 7.3, 33-48.

Rudolph, Elisabeth. 1996. *Contrast: Adversative and Concessive Relations and Their Expressions in English, German, Spanish and Portuguese on Sentence Level and Text Level.* Berlin & New York: Mouton de Gruyter.

Sacks, Harvey. 1987. On the preference for agreement and contiguity in sequences in conversation. In Graham Button, John R.E. Lee (eds.), *Talk and Social Organisation*, 54-69. Clevedon: Multilingual.

Sanders, Ted J. M., Wilbert P.M. Spooren, Leo G.M. Noordman. 1993. Coherence relations in a cognitive theory of discourse representation. *Cognitive Linguistics* 4.2, 93-133.

Schegloff, Emanuel A., Gail Jefferson and Harvey Sacks. 1977. The Preference for Self-Correction in the Organization of

Repair in Conversation. *Language* 53.2, 361-382.

Sheldon, Amy. 1974. The Role of Parallel Function in the Acquisition of Relative Clauses in English. *Journal of Verbal Learning and Verbal Behavior* 13, 272-281.

Schiffrin, Deborah. 1987. *Discourse Markers*. Cambridge: Cambridge University Press.

Shaw, Samuel. 1969[1687]. *Grammatica Anglo-Romana*. London: Michael Johnson.

Spenader, Jennifer and Anna Lobanova. 2009. Reliable discourse markers for contrast relations. Proceedings of the 8th International Conference on Computational Semantics, 210-221.

Sperber, Dan and Deirdre Wilson. 1986. *Relevance: Communication and Cognition*. Oxford: Blackwell.

Stern, Gustav. 1968[1931]. *Meaning and Change of Meaning: With Special Reference to the English Language*. Bloomington: Indiana University Press.

Stojanova-Jovceva, Stanka. 1979. Untersuchungen zur Stilistik der Nebensatze in der deutschen Gegenwartssprache. *Beiträge zur Geschichte der deutschen Sprache und Literatur* 100, 40-178.

Stubbs, Michael. 1983. *Discourse Analysis: The Sociolinguistic Analysis of Natural Language*. Oxford: Basil Blackwell.

Sweetser, Eve E. 1982. Root and epistemic modals: Causality in two worlds. *Berkeley Linguistics Society* 8, 484-507.

Sweetser, Eve E. 1990. *From Etymology to Pragmatics: Metaphorical and Cultural Aspects of Semantic Structure*.

Cambridge: Cambridge University Press.

Taylor, John. 1995. *Linguistic Categorization: Prototypes in Linguistic Theory*. Oxford: Clarendon Press.

Thompson, Sandra A. 1987. 'Concessive' as a discourse relation in expository written English. In Brian D. Joseph and Arnold M. Zwicky, (eds.), *A Festschrift for Ilse Lehiste,* 64-73. (Working Papers in *Linguistics* 35.) Ohio: State University.

Traugott, Elizabeth C. 1982. From propositional to textual and expressive meanings: Some semantic-pragmatic aspects of grammaticalization. In Winfred Lehmann and Yakov Malkiel (eds.), *Directions for Historical Linguistics,* 245-71. Amsterdam: John Benjamins.

Traugott, Elizabeth C. 1986. Is internal semantic-pragmatic reconstruction possible? In Caroline Duncan-Rose and Theo Vennemann (eds.), *On Language: Rhetorica, Phonologica, Syntactica: A Festschrift for Robert P. Stockwell from his Friends and Colleageus.* London: Routledge.

Traugott, Elizabeth C. 1988. Pragmatic strengthening and grammaticalization. *Berkeley Linguistics Society* 14, 406-416.

Traugott, Elizabeth C. 1989. On the rise of epistemic meanings in English: An example of subjectification in semantic change. *Language* 65.1, 31-55.

Traugott, Elizabeth C. 1992. Syntax. In Richard Hogg (ed.), *The Cambridge History of The English Language*, 4 vols. Vol. 1, 168-289. Cambridge & New York: Cambridge University Press.

Traugott, Elizabeth C. 1997. The discourse connective *after all*: A historical pragmatic account. Paper presented at the 10th International Congress of Linguistics, July 1997, Paris.

Traugott, Elizabeth C. 1999. The rhetoric of counter-expectation in semantic change: A study in subjectification. In Peter Koch and Andreas Blank (eds.), *Historical Semantics and Cognition*, 177-196. Berlin & New York: Mouton de Gruyter.

Traugott, Elizabeth C. and Ekkehard König. 1991. The semantics-pragmatics of grammaticalization revisited. In Elizabeth C. Traugott and Bernd Heine (eds.), *Approaches to Grammaticalization*, 2 vols. Vol. 1, 189-218. Amsterdam: John Benjamins.

van der Auwera, Johan (ed.) 1998. *Adverbial Constructions in the Languages of Europe*. Berlin/New York: Mouton de Gruyter.

Verhagen, Arie. 2000. Concessive implies causality, though in some other space. In Elizabeth Couper-Kuhlen and Bernd Kortmann (eds.), *Cause, Condition, Concession, Contrast: Cognitive and Discourse Perspectives*, 360-380. Berlin & New York: Mouton de Gruyter.

Wiechmann, Daniel and Elma Kerz. 2013. The positioning of concessive adverbial clauses in English: Assessing the importance of discourse-pragmatic and processing-based constraints. *English Language and Linguistics* 17.1, 1-23.

# Appendix 1

Transcription Conventions Used in the MICASE

<PAUSE DUR=:05> Pauses of 4 seconds or longer are timed to the nearest second such as <P: 05>

<EVENT DESC=LAUGH> or <EVENT DESC=LAUGH WHO=S2> All laughter is marked. Speaker ID is not marked if current speaker laughs such as <LAUGH>, <S8 LAUGH>, <SS LAUGH>, etc.

Embedded and overlapped utterance (<OVERLAP> tag within an embedded utterance) Backchannel cues or unsuccessful interruptions that overlap with the main speaker's speech. [S3: Text of embedded speech that is overlapped is surrounded by speaker ID and square brackets.]

# Appendix 2

## Transcript ID and Its Hits in the MICASE Used for Discourse Analysis of *Though*

| Transcript ID | Hits |
|---|---|
| ADV700JU023 | 4 |
| ADV700JU047 | 10 |
| DIS175JU081 | 5 |
| DIS495JU119 | 1 |
| LAB200JU018 | 5 |
| LAB175SU026 | 27 |
| LAB175SU032 | 10 |
| LAB175SU033 | 5 |
| I AB500SU044 | 5 |
| LES215MU056 | 1 |
| LES320SU085 | 4 |
| LES565SU137 | 5 |
| LES220SU140 | 8 |
| MTG425JG004 | 4 |
| MTG400MX008 | 6 |
| MTG999ST015 | 6 |
| MTG485SG142 | 4 |
| OFC578SG037 | 3 |
| OFC150MU042 | 12 |
| OFC575MU046 | 13 |
| OFC270MG048 | 4 |
| OFC115SU060 | 12 |

| Transcript ID | Hits |
|---|---|
| OFC105SU068 | 2 |
| OFC355SU094 | 5 |
| OFC280SU109 | 8 |
| OFC195SU116 | 8 |
| OFC175JU145 | 3 |
| OFC320SU153 | 3 |
| SEM475JU084 | 9 |
| SEM300MU100 | 13 |
| SGR385SU057 | 15 |
| SGR999MX115 | 25 |
| SGR175SU123 | 20 |
| SGR200JU125 | 8 |
| SGR175MU126 | 7 |
| SGR195SU127 | 17 |
| SGR565SU144 | 16 |
| SGR999SU146 | 6 |
| STP125JG050 | 8 |
| SVC999MX104 | 13 |
| SVC999MX148 | 6 |
| **Total** | **335** |

# Index

## A



## B



## C

## L



## M



## N



## O



## P



## Q



## R



## S

## T



## U



## V



## W



## X



## Y

Synchronic and Diachronic Analysis of English Concessives

# CONCESSION IN DISCOURSE